HONITON LACE
THE VISUAL APPROACH

HONITON LACE
THE VISUAL APPROACH

Elsie Luxton and
Yusai Fukuyama

B. T. Batsford Ltd · London

Patterns 1–22
   Designed by Elsie Luxton
   Worked by Elsie Luxton

Patterns 23–40
   Designed by Yusai Fukuyama
   Worked by Saikoh Takano

Illustrated by Yusai Fukuyama
Photographed by Yusai Fukuyama

© Elsie Luxton and Yusai Fukuyama 1988
First published 1988

ISBN 0 7134 5936 0

Filmset by Lasertext Ltd, Longford Trading Estate,
Thomas Street, Stretford, Manchester M32 0JT.
and printed by Anchor Brendon Ltd. Tiptree, Essex
for the publishers
B. T. Batsford Ltd.
4 Fitzhardinge Street
London W1H 0AH

Contents

Introduction

I present this my third book on Honiton lacemaking in conjunction with a past student and friend for many years, Yusai Fukuyama from Tokyo. I am grateful to him for his help and experience.

With the ever increasing number of lacemakers worldwide, his easy-to-follow diagrams produced here, break down all language barriers – indeed, many lacemakers prefer diagrams to the written instruction.

My patterns are all new designs and include both flat and raised work; each pattern has an actual size pricking, line drawing, and diagram giving the number of pairs used. All patterns in this book have been worked with 180 cotton thread: the finest obtainable at present. Photographs of the finished lace are given, and to help the lacemaker when working the pattern, we have also now shown the reverse side of the work.

I still consider Honiton Lace to be the finest and queen of all English laces.

Elsie Luxton

What is this new visual approach?

People admire the art of Honiton lace and believe it to be one of the most elegant and beautiful laces in the world. Yet many think it is a lace which is too difficult for them to make themselves; some think their eyesight is not good enough to see the fine threads, whilst others believe the techniques are too difficult for them to understand.

This book has been planned so that a lacemaker who has a basic knowledge of bobbin lacemaking can easily understand the patterns by studying the diagrams and photographs. As there is no written description with the patterns, it is anticipated that language will not be a barrier and hence the book may be used by lacemakers in any country, irrespective of the language they may use.

When making Honiton lace, the lacemaker is looking at the wrong side of the work, so every design in this book has a photograph of the right and wrong side of the lace – so the lacemakers do not need to reverse the usual photograph of the lace in their minds.

The authors have tried to show that Honiton lacemaking may be easily understood from the illustrations. The working order is shown by the arrows.

Yusai Fukuyama

How to use this book

1 All photographs of the finished work are shown from page 14 to 20 so that comparisons can be easily made and the desired design chosen.

2 Every design is shown in a double-page spread and is illustrated by a photograph of the right side, a photograph of the wrong side, a diagram showing the direction of working, the number of pairs required, and a pricking.

3 Each design has the same numbering for all the illustrations, e.g.

   -the right side photograph 1-a,
   -the wrong side photograph 1-b,
   -the working order 1-c,
   -the number of pairs 1-d,
   -and the pricking 1-e.

4 The photograph of the wrong side of the lace is shown so that the lacemaker has a direct comparison with his/her work and the author's work during the making of the lace.

5 The patterns have been worked in 180/2 cotton thread and so the number of threads in the diagrams refers to 180 thread.
   When a coarse thread was required No. 50 sewing cotton was used.

6 In the diagram the direction of working is shown by the arrows and the number of pairs of bobbins required for each part is indicated by the number i.e. 5 = 5 pairs or 10 bobbins.
   The coarse pair is shown as C, e.g. 6 + C means 6 pairs of bobbins and a coarse pair.
   The filling is shown as F, e.g. F6 means Filling 6.
   The rib is shown as R, e.g. R5 means 5 pairs rib.

7 All prickings in this book are shown in the actual size.

Yusai Fukuyama

Comment Utiliser ce Livre

1 Toutes les photos des travaux finis se trouvent page 14 à 20 pour faciliter le choix d'un modèle.

2 Chaque modèle est présenté sur une double page qui donne une photo de l'endroit et une photo de l'envers du travail, un schema qui donne le nombre de paires de fuseaux et le sens du travail, un carton.

3 Tous les modèles sont présentés dans le même ordre;
     1-a: vue de l'endroit
     1-b: vue de l'envers
     1-c: sens du travail
     1-d: nombre de paires de fuseaux
     1-e: carton

4 La photo de l'envers permet une comparaison du travail avec le modèle pendant la réalisation de la dentelle.

5 Tous les modèles sont réalisés avec du fil 180/2;quand un fil plus gros est nécessaire du fil a coudre no. 50 est utilisé.

6 Sur les schémas le sens du travail est indiqué par des flèches et le nombre de paires de fuseaux nécessaire pour chaque partie est désignée par un nombre.
Exemple: 5 = 5 paires ou 10 fuseaux.
         La paire de fil gros est désignée par C.
Exemple: 6 + c Signifie 6 paires de fuseaux plus une paire de fil gros.
         Les parties pleines sont désignées par F.
Exemple: F6 signifie = partie pleine 6 La côte est désignée par R.
Exemple: R5 signifié côte de 5 paires.

7 Tous les cartons sont grandeur nature.

Algemene aanwijzingen

1 Alle foto's van het gekloste werk staan afgedrukt van bladzijde 14 tot 20, zodat het gemakkelijk is een vergelijking te maken en het gewenste ontwerp te kiezen.

2 Elk ontwerp is afgedrukt over twee pagina's en wordt verduidelijkt door een foto van de goede kant, een foto van de achterkant, een technische tekening, waarop aangegeven het benodigde aantal paren en de werkrichting, en een prikpatroon.

3 Elk onderdeel van de toelichting van de ontwerpen heeft hetzelfde nummer b.v. de foto van de goede kant 1-a, de foto van de achterkant 1-b, de werktekening 1-c, het aantal paren 1-d, en het prikpatroon 1-e.

4 De foto van de achterzijde van het kant is opgenomen, opdat de klosser(ster) zijn/haar werk tijdens het klossen kan vergelijken met het werk van de schrijver/ster.

5 De patronen zijn geklost met katoen 180/2 en het aantal draden in de technische tekening is gebaseerd op dikte 180. Daar waar een contourdraad nodig was, is katoenen naaigaren No. 50 gebruikt.

6 In de technische tekening wordt de werkrichting aangegeven door de pijlen en het aantal klosjes, dat nodig is voor elk deel, wordt aangegeven door het getal b.v. 5 = 5 paar of 10 klosjes, Het contourpaar wordt aangegeven door een C b.v. 6 + C betekent 6 paar klosjes en een contourpaar.
De vulling wordt aangegeven met F, b.v. F6 betekent vulling 6. De rib wordt aangegeven met R, b.v. R5 betekent een rib van 5 paren.

7 Alle prikpatronen in dit boek zijn afgedrukt op ware grootte.

Wie man dieses Buch benutzt

1 Zur Veranschaulichung und leichteren Wahl des zu klöppelnden Motivs sind die Fotos der fertigen Spitzen auf den Seiten 14 bis 20 abgebildet.

2 Jeder Entwurf wird auf einer Doppelseite gezeigt, illustriert durch ein Foto von Vorder- und Rückseite der Spitze, einer technischen Zeichnung mit Angabe der erforderlichen Klöppel, der Arbeitsverlaufs sowie dem Klöppelbrief.

3 Zu jedem Entwurf erhalten die dazugehörigen Abbildungen durchweg die gleiche Nummerierung, z.B. Foto der Vorderseite der Spitze l-a, Rückseite l-b, Arbeitsanleitung l-c, Anzahl der Klöppel l-d, Musterbrief l-e.

4 Im Foto wird die Rückseite (linke Seite) der Spitze gezeigt, damit während des Klöppelns ein direkter Vergleich möglich ist.

5 Die Muster wurden mit Baumwollgarn 180/2 geklöppelt, die Anzahl der Fäden im Muster beziehen sich daher stets auf Garnstärke 180. Als Konturfaden wurde Nähgarn Nr. 50 benutzt.

6 In der technischen Zeichnung wird der Arbeitsverlauf durch Pfeile angegeben, die Anzahl der für die einzelnen Teile erforderlichen Klöppelpaare wird durch entsprechende Zahlen angegeben, z.B. 5 = 5 Paare (10 Klöppel).
Der Konturfaden wird mit 'C' bezeichnet, so bedeutet 6 + C = 6 Klöppelpaare sowie 1 Paar Konturfaden.
Füllungen sind mit 'F' bezeichnet, so daß F6 bedeutet: Fülling 6.
Die Rippe wird mit 'R' bezeichnet, R5 bedeutet 5 Paare für die Rippe.

7 Alle Briefe sind in Originalgröße abgebildet.

Richtlijnen

1 Alle uitgewerkte stukken zijn afgebeeld vanaf blz. 14 tot 20. Om de vergelijking te vergemakkelijken is de rechter- en averechte zijde gefotografeerd.

2 Elk uitgewerkt stuk is afgebeeld op een dubbel blad met bijgaande foto van rechter- en averechte zijde. Een diagram geeft het aantal te gebruiken klossen aan en richt- lijnen voor uitvoering en prikking.

3 Elk patroon draagt hetzelfde nummer voor de illustraties, v.b. de rechter zijde van de foto 1-a, de averechte zijde 1-b, de manier van werken 1-c, het aantal klossen 1-d, en de prikking 1-e.

4 De reden voor het fotograferen van de averechte zijde van de kant is om het de kantwerkster gemakkelijker te maken om haar (of zijn) werk tevergelijken met dat van de schijver.

5 De patronen zijn uitgewerkt in katoen Nr. 80/2, de nummers van het garen in de dia- grams verwijzen naar Nr. 180.
Wanneer een dikker soort garen gebruikt werd refereren wij naar stikgaren Nr. 50.

6 In de diagram is de richting waarin moet gewerkt worden aangegeven door pijlen. De nodige klossen voor elk te werken deel is aangegeven door nummers v.b. 5 = 5 paren of 10 klossen.
Het paar met de dikke draad is C, v.b. 6 = C betekent 6 paren en één paar met dikke draad.
De vulling is voorgeteld door F, v.b. F6 is vulling 6.
Het ribbetje is voorgesteld ddor R. v.b.; R5 betekend 5 paren rib.

7 Alle prikkingen in het boek komen voor in werkelijke grootte.

Elsie Luxton's Patterns

1 Shell

Fig. 1-a   right side photograph

Fig. 1-c   working order

Fig. 1-b   wrong side photograph

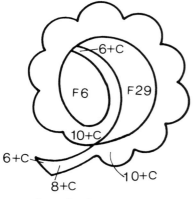

Fig. 1-d   number of pairs

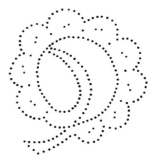

Fig. 1-e   pricking

2 Forget-me-not

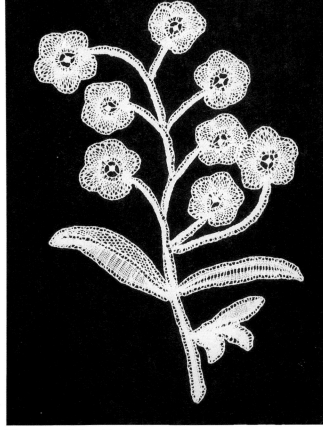

Fig. 2-a   right side photograph

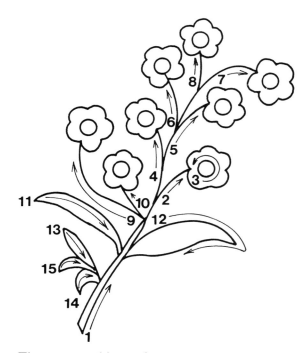

Fig. 2-c   working order

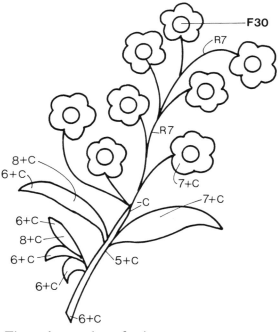

Fig. 2-d   number of pairs

Fig. 2-b   wrong side photograph

Fig. 2-e   pricking

3 Maze

Fig. 3-a   right side photograph

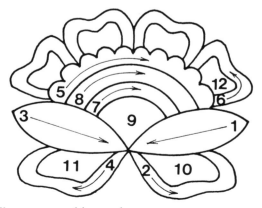

Fig. 3-c   working order

26

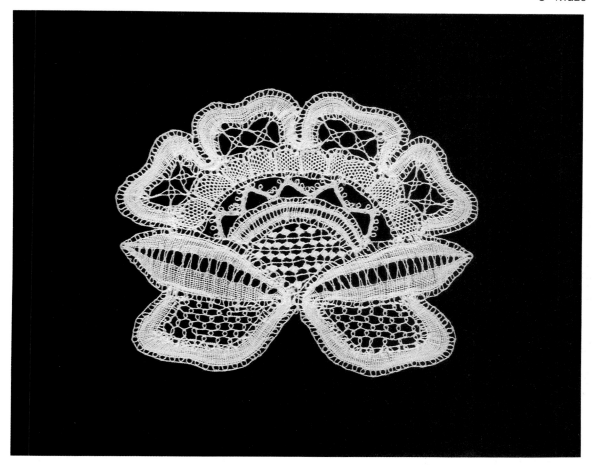

Fig. 3-b   wrong side photograph

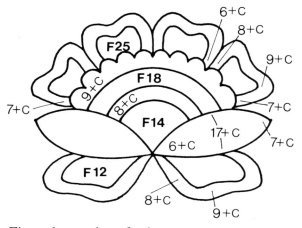

Fig. 3-d   number of pairs

Fig. 3-e   pricking

4 Estuary

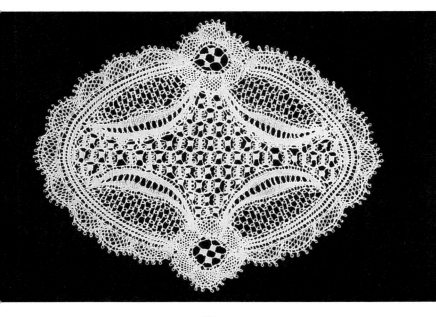

Fig. 4-a   right
side photograph

Fig. 4-c   working order

Fig. 4-b   wrong side photograph

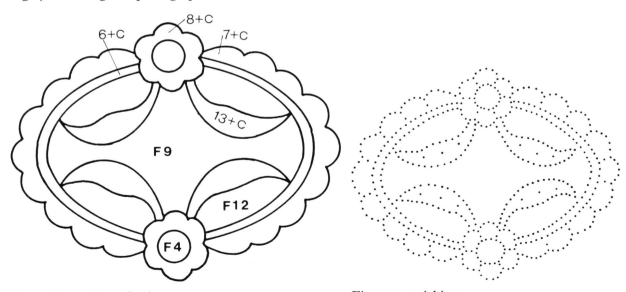

Fig. 4-d   number of pairs

Fig. 4-e   pricking

29

5 Blossom

Fig. 5-a right side photograph

Fig. 5-c working order

Fig. 5-b   wrong side photograph

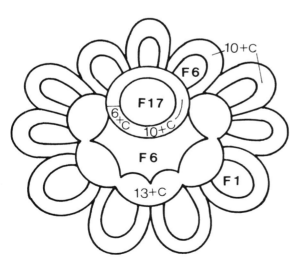

Fig. 5-d   number of pairs

Fig. 5-e   pricking

6 Butterfly

Fig. 6-a   right side photograph

Fig. 6-c   working order

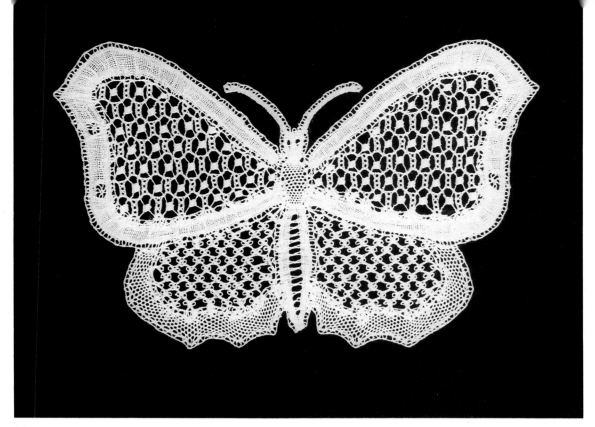

Fig. 6-b   wrong side photograph

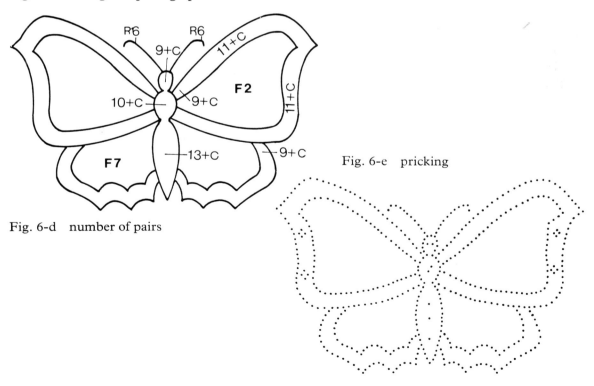

Fig. 6-d   number of pairs

Fig. 6-e   pricking

7 Brooch Pattern

Fig. 7-a right side photograph

Fig. 7-c working order

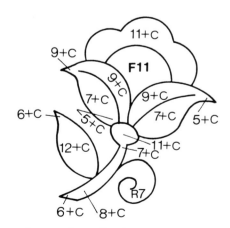

Fig. 7-d number of pairs

Fig. 7-b wrong
side photograph

Fig. 7-e pricking

8 Pride

Fig. 8-a   right side photograph

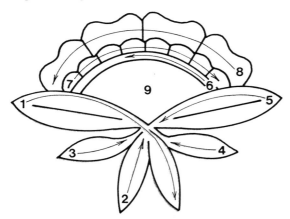

Fig. 8-c   working order

Fig. 8-b   wrong side photograph

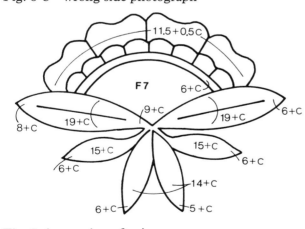

Fig. 8-d   number of pairs

Fig. 8-e   pricking

9 Sampler

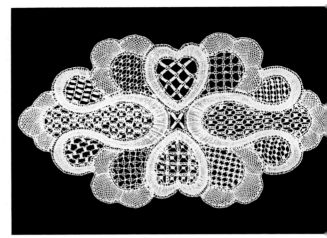

Fig. 9-a right side photograph

Fig. 9-c working order

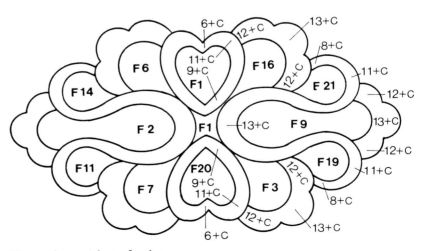

Fig. 9-d number of pairs

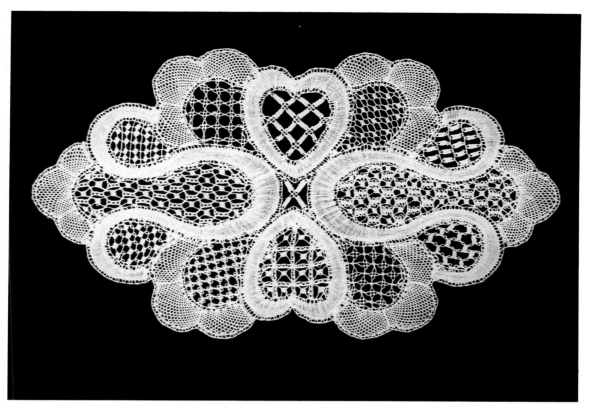

Fig. 9-b   wrong side photograph

Fig. 9-e   pricking

10 Handkerchief

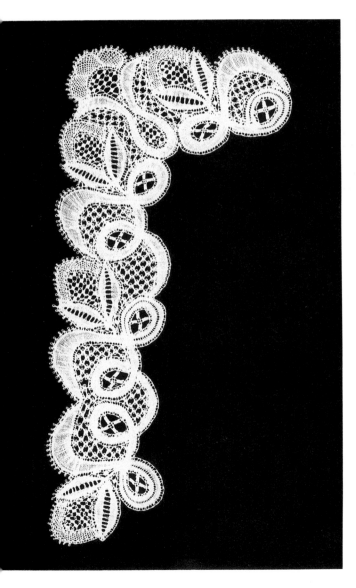

Fig. 10-a   right side photograph

Fig. 10-c   working order

6+C 13+C 10+C
F11
F1 15+C F11
10+C
10+C 6+C
9+C
F 7
8+C
15+C
6+C
13+C
10+C
6+C
10+C 6+C

Fig. 10-d   number of pairs

Fig. 10-b   wrong side photograph

Fig. 10-e   pricking

11 Taw edging

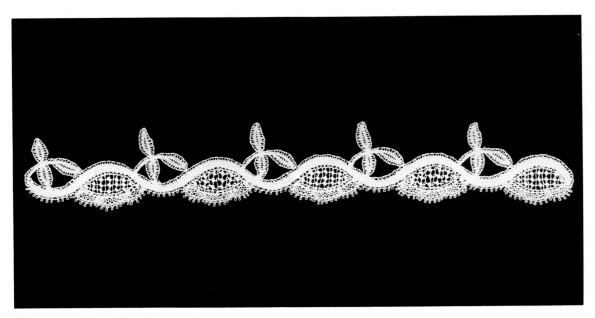

Fig. 11-a   right side photograph

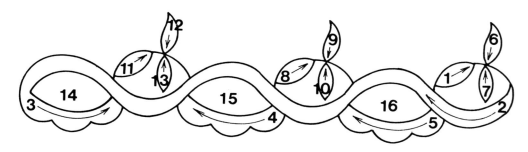

Fig. 11-c   working order

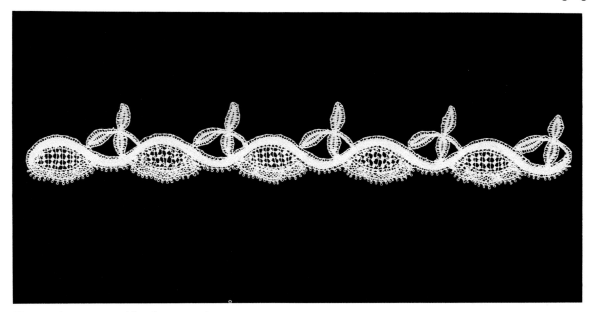

Fig. 11-b   wrong side photograph

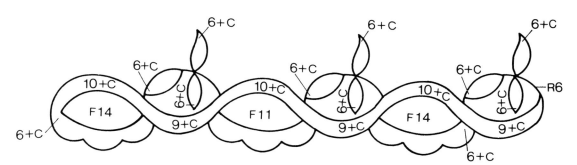

Fig. 11-d   number of pairs

Fig. 11-e   pricking

12 Dart edging

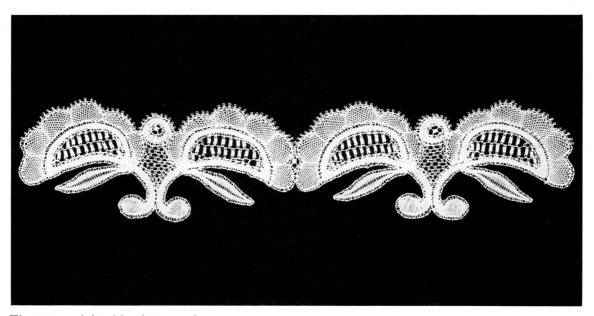

Fig. 12-a   right side photograph

Fig. 12-c   working order

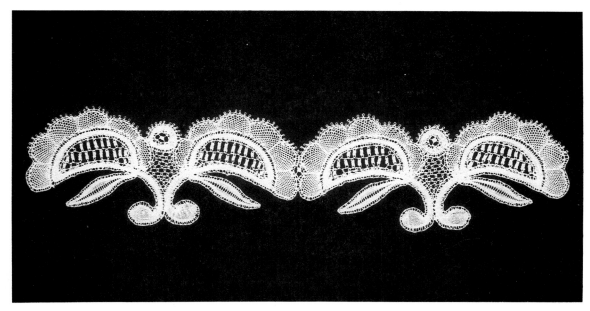

Fig. 12-b   wrong side photograph

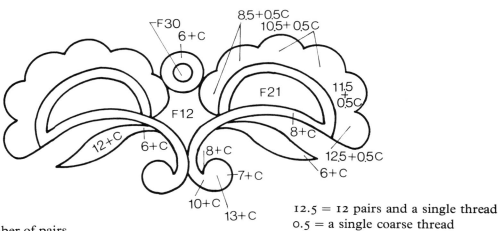

Fig. 12-d   number of pairs

12.5 = 12 pairs and a single thread
0.5 = a single coarse thread

Fig. 12-e   pricking

45

13 Lilies

Fig. 13-a   right side photograph

Fig. 13-c   working order

Fig. 13-b wrong side photograph

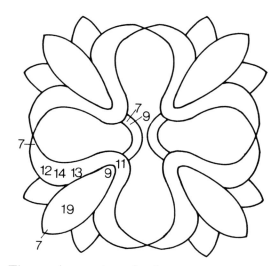

Fig. 13-d number of pairs

Fig. 13-e pricking

All numbers include one coarse pair

14 Brooch pattern

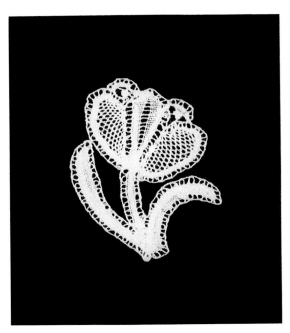

Fig. 14-a   right side photograph

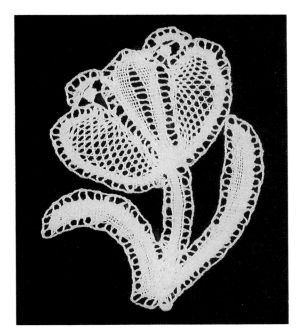

Fig. 14-b   wrong side photograph

Fig. 14-c   working order

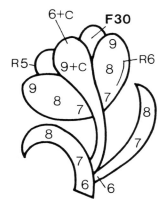

Fig. 14-d   number of pairs

Fig. 14-e   pricking

15 Shell

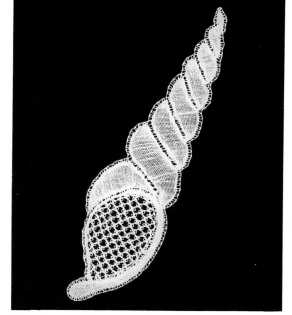

Fig. 15-a   right side photograph

Fig. 15-b   wrong side photograph

Fig. 15-c   working order

Fig. 15-d   number of pairs

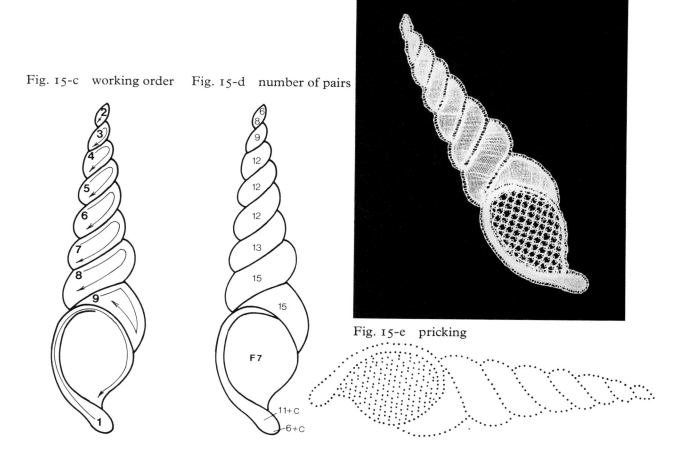

Fig. 15-e   pricking

49

16 Leaf

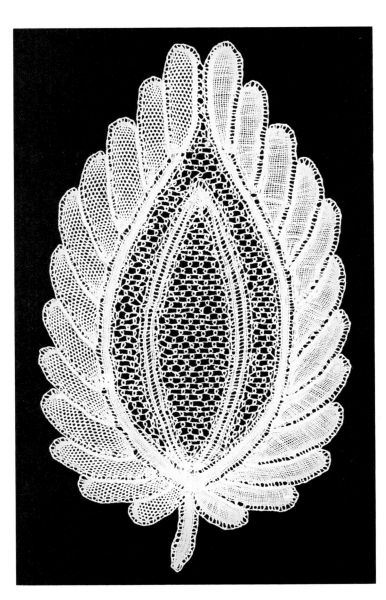

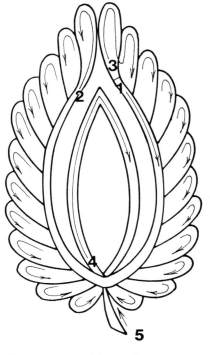

Fig. 16-a   right side photograph

Fig. 16-c   working order

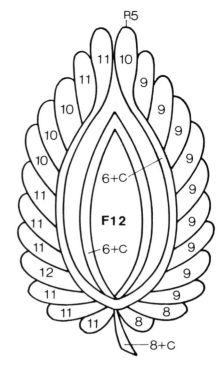

Fig. 16-d   number of pairs

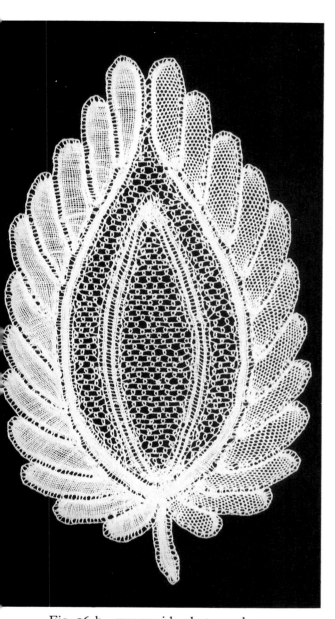

Fig. 16-b   wrong side photograph

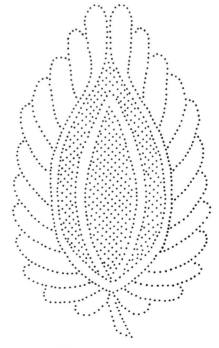

Fig. 16-e   pricking

17 Snowdrop

Fig. 17-a   right side photograph

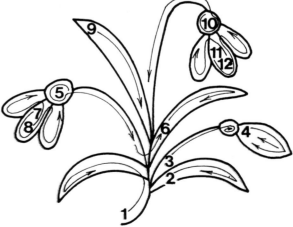

Fig. 17-c   working order

Fig. 17-b   wrong side photograph

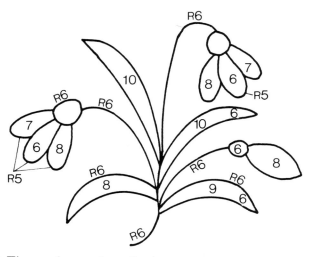

Fig. 17-d   number of pairs

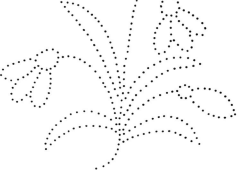

Fig. 17-e   pricking

18 Reed design

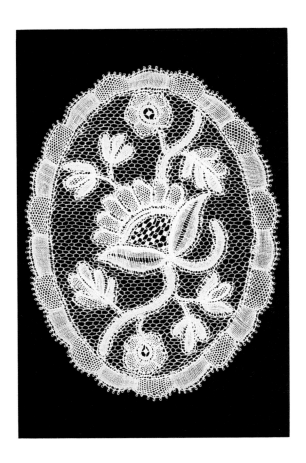

Fig. 18-a right side photograph

Fig. 18-c working order

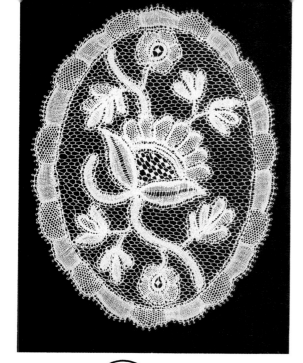

Fig. 18-b   wrong side photograph

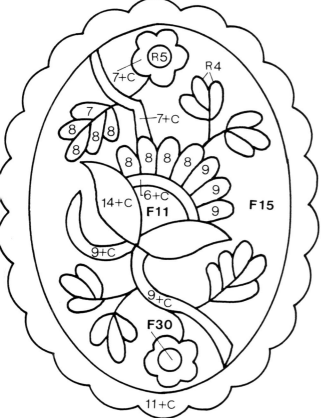

Fig. 18-d   number of pairs

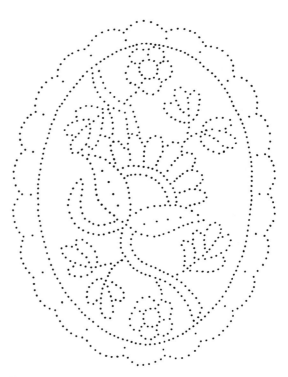

Fig. 18-e   pricking

19 Rolduc

Fig. 19-a   right side photograph

Fig. 19-b wrong side photograph

Fig. 19-c working order

Fig. 19-d number of pairs

Fig. 19-e pricking

20 Goulden design

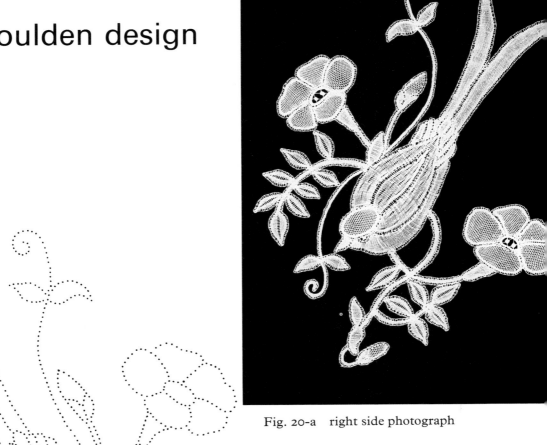

Fig. 20-a   right side photograph

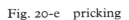

Fig. 20-e   pricking

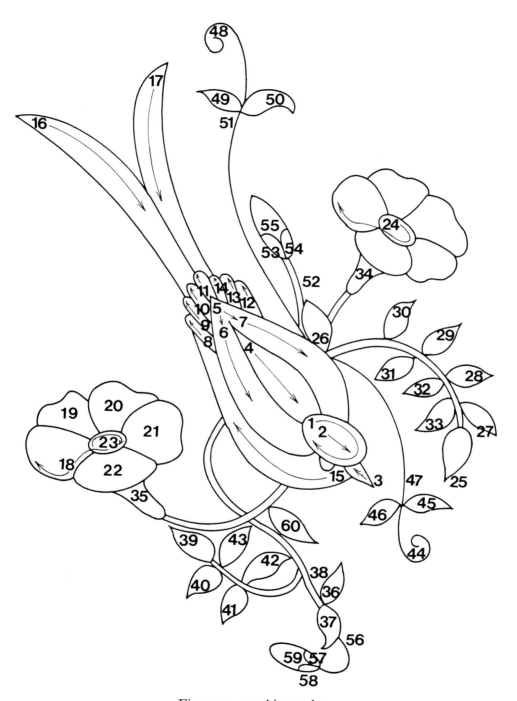

Fig. 20-c   working order

60

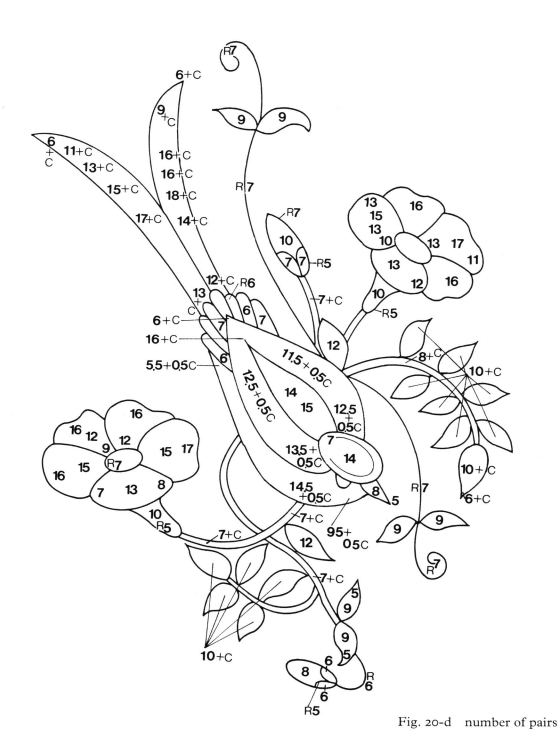

Fig. 20-b   wrong side photograph

Fig. 20-d   number of pairs

21 Grape

Fig. 21-a right side photograph

Fig. 21-b wrong side photograph

Fig. 21-c   working order

Fig. 21-d   number of pairs

Fig. 21-e   pricking

22 Roses

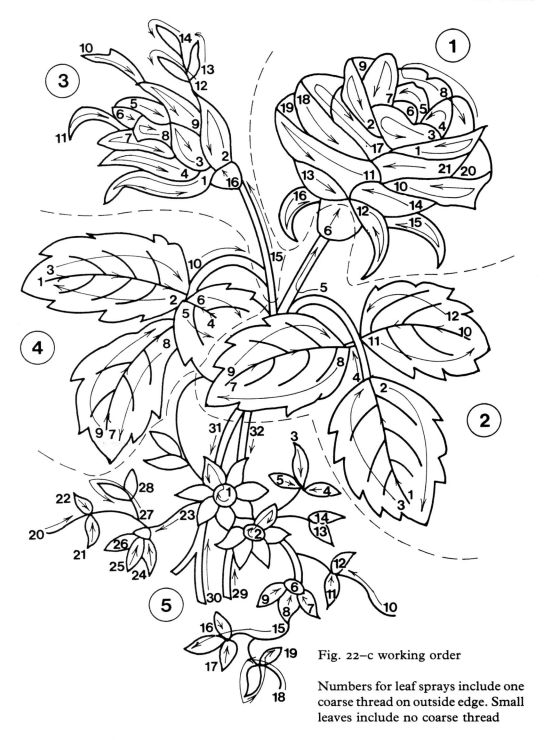

Fig. 22–c working order

Numbers for leaf sprays include one coarse thread on outside edge. Small leaves include no coarse thread

Fig. 22-a right side photograph

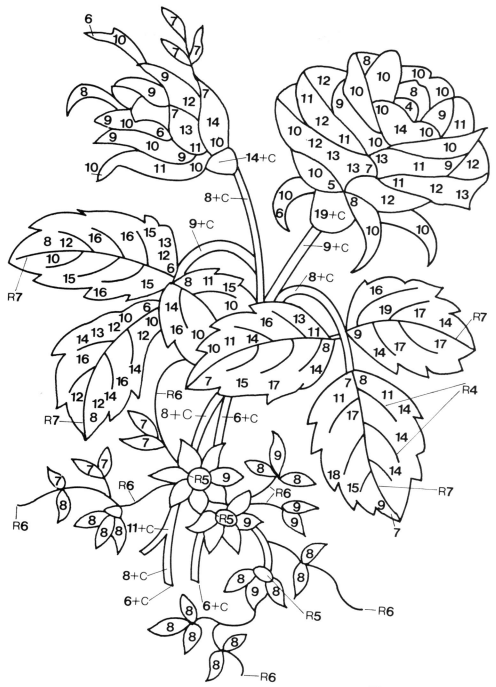

Fig. 22-d   number of pairs

Fig. 22-b   wrong side photograph

Fig. 22-e   pricking

Yusai Fukuyama's Patterns

23 Maple

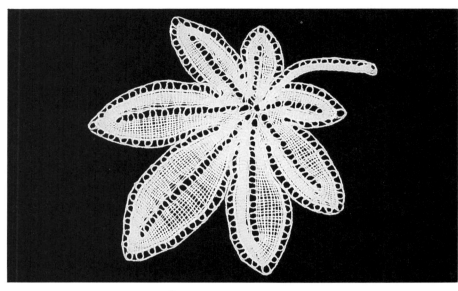

Fig. 23-a   right
side photograph

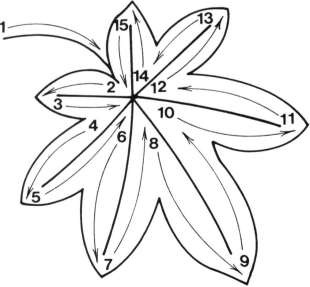

Fig. 23-c   working order

Fig. 23-b wrong
side photograph

5.5 + 0.5C

5.5 + 0.5C

6.5 + 0.5C

6.5 = 6 pairs and a single thread
0.5C = a single coarse thread

6.5 + 0.5C

7.5 + 0.5C

Fig. 23-d   number of pairs

Fig. 23-e   pricking

24 Iris

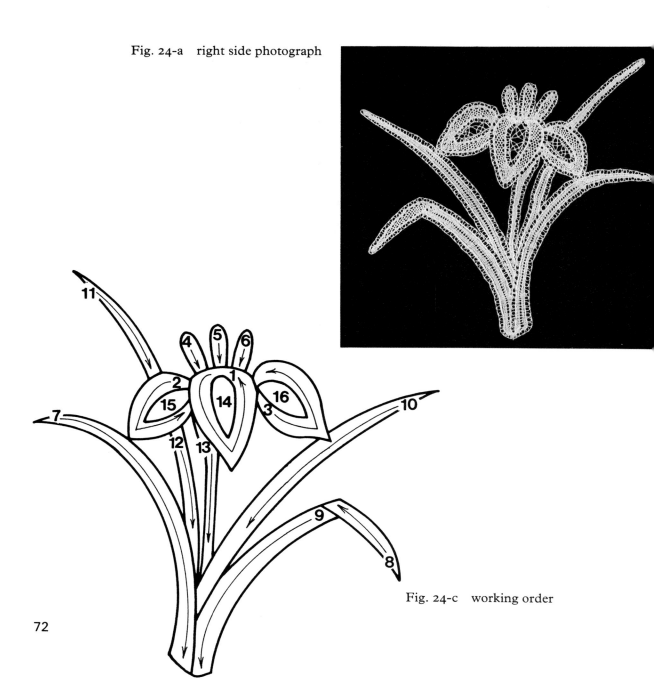

Fig. 24-a   right side photograph

Fig. 24-c   working order

Fig. 24-b   wrong
side photograph

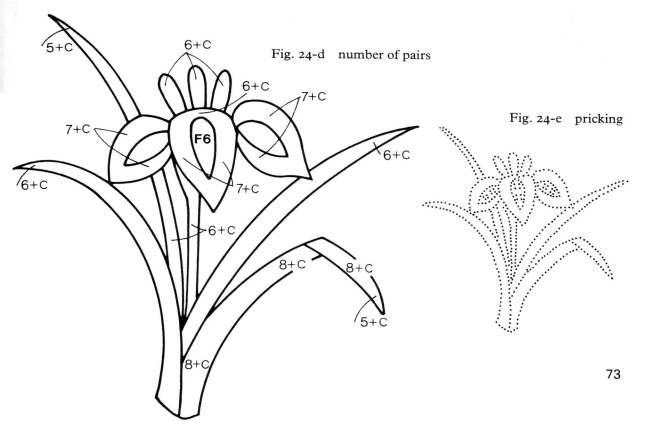

Fig. 24-d   number of pairs

5+C
6+C
6+C
7+C
7+C
F6
6+C
7+C
6+C
6+C
8+C   8+C
5+C
8+C

Fig. 24-e   pricking

25 Butterfly

Fig. 25-a   right side photograph

Fig. 25-c   working order

Fig. 25-b   wrong side photograph

10.5 = 10 pairs and a single thread
0.5 C = a single coarse thread

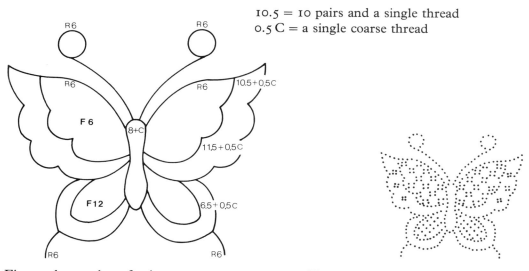

Fig. 25-d   number of pairs

Fig. 25-e   pricking

26 Crane

Fig. 26-a   right
side photograph

Fig. 26-c   working order

Fig. 26-b   wrong side photograph

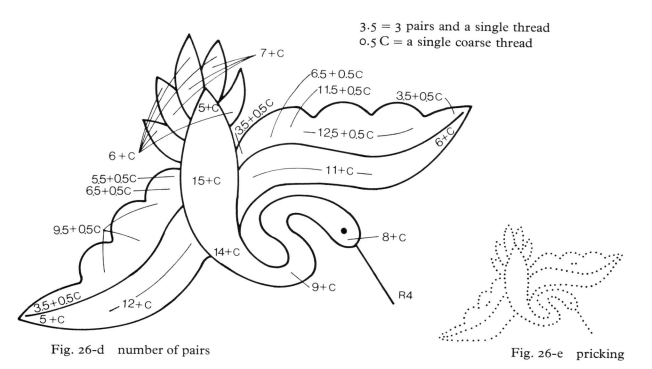

3.5 = 3 pairs and a single thread
0.5 C = a single coarse thread

7 + C

6.5 + 0.5C
11.5 + 0.5C
3.5 + 0.5C

5 + C
3.5 + 0.5C
—12.5 + 0.5C—
6 + C

6 + C
5.5 + 0.5C
6.5 + 0.5C
15 + C
— 11 + C —

9.5 + 0.5C

8 + C

14 + C

9 + C

R4

3.5 + 0.5C
5 + C
— 12 + C —

Fig. 26-d   number of pairs

Fig. 26-e   pricking

77

27 Cherry blossoms

Fig. 27-c   working order

Fig. 27-a   right side photograph

Fig. 27-b   wrong side photograph

5.5 + 1.5C

8.5 + 1.5C

8 + C

8 + C

R 5 + C

5 + C

7 + C

7 + C

6 + C

7 + C

5.5 + 1.5C

5 + C

8.5 + 1.5C

7 + C
6 + C

7.5 + 1.5C

5.5 + 1.5C

8 + C

3 + C   6 + C

Fig. 27-d   number of pairs

Fig. 27-e   pricking

79

28 Oriental flower

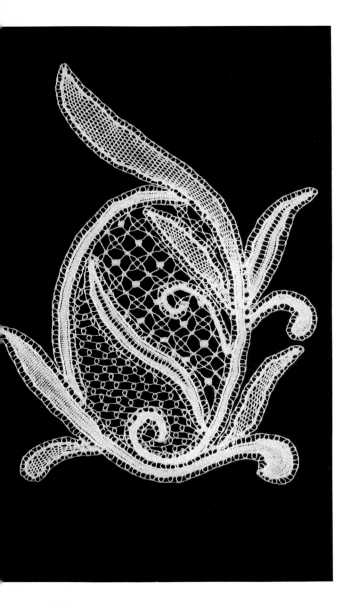

Fig. 28-a   right side photograph

Fig. 28-c   working order

Fig. 28-b   wrong side photograph

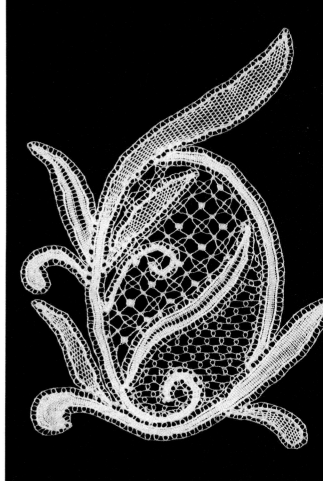

6+C

13+C

9+C

6+C

7+C

6+C

F6

10+C

6+C

9+C

9+C

6+C

3+C

2+C

F23

(R6)

8+C

7+C

9+C

3+C

6+C

F12

7+C

6+C

8+C

10+C

3+C   7+C

9+C

5+C

6+C

6+C

5+C

8+C

12+C

3+C

7+C

9+C

Fig. 28-d   number of pairs

Fig. 28-e   pricking

81

29 Plum tree

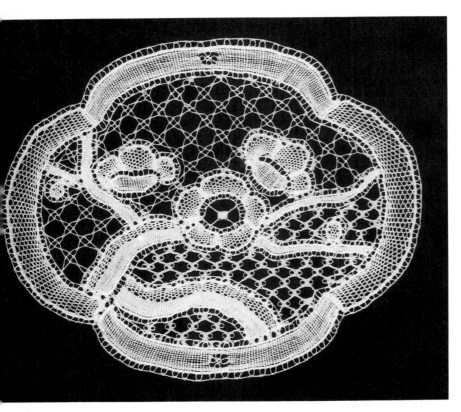

Fig. 29-a   right side photograph

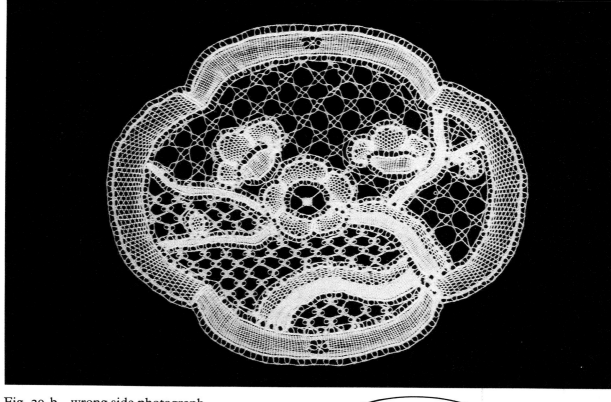

Fig. 29-b   wrong side photograph

Fig. 29-d   number of pairs

Fig. 29-c   working order

Fig. 29-e   pricking

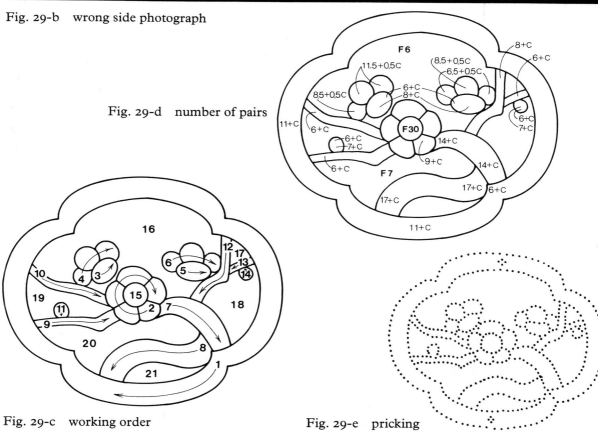

83

30 Chidori

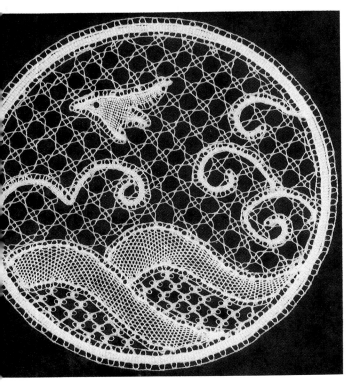

Fig. 30-a   right side photograph

Fig. 30-c   working order

Fig. 30-b   wrong side photograph

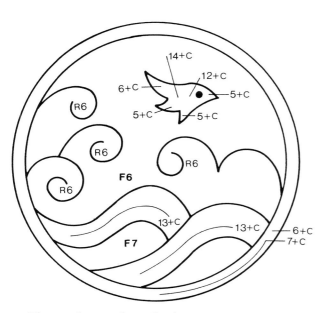

Fig. 30-d   number of pairs

Fig. 30-e   pricking

31 Ivy

Fig. 31-a   right side photograph

Fig. 31-c   working order

Fig. 31-b   wrong side photograph

5.5 = 5 pairs and a single thread
0.5 C = a single coarse thread

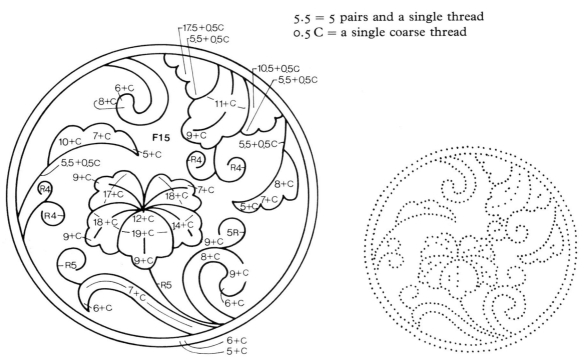

Fig. 31-d   number of pairs

Fig. 31-e   pricking

32 Butterfly

Fig. 32-b wrong side photograph

Fig. 32-c working order

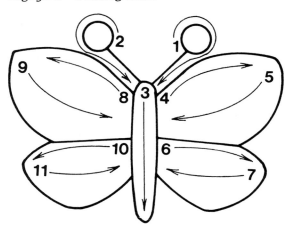

Fig. 32-a right side photograph

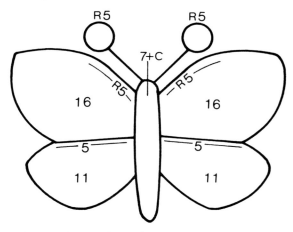

Fig. 32-d number of pairs

Fig. 32-e pricking

33 Swallow

Fig. 33-a   right side photograph

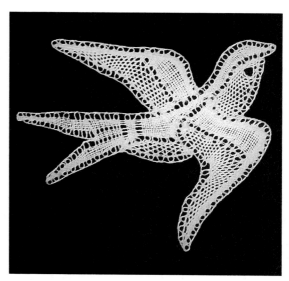

Fig. 33-b   wrong side photograph

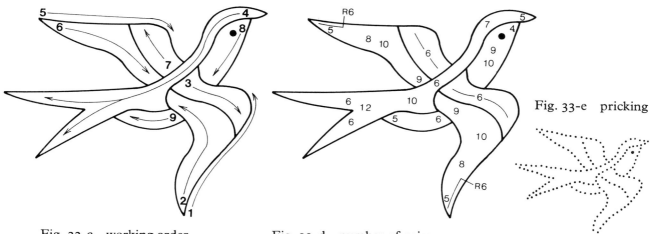

Fig. 33-c   working order

Fig. 33-d   number of pairs

Fig. 33-e   pricking

34 Chrysanthemum

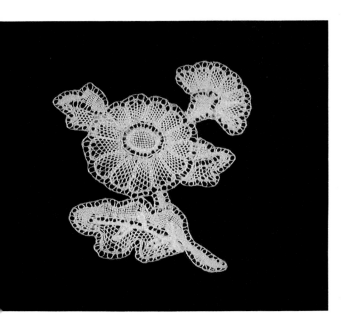

Fig. 34-a   right side photograph

Fig. 34-b   wrong side photograph

Fig. 34-c   working order

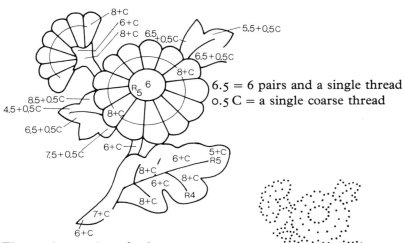

8+C
6+C
8+C   6.5+0.5C
5.5+0.5C
6.5+0.5C
8+C
R5   6
8.5+0.5C
4.5+0.5C
8+C
6.5+0.5C
6+C
7.5+0.5C
5+C
R5
6+C
8+C
6+C   8+C
8+C   R4
7+C
6+C

6.5 = 6 pairs and a single thread
0.5 C = a single coarse thread

Fig. 34-d   number of pairs

Fig. 34-e   pricking

35 Rose

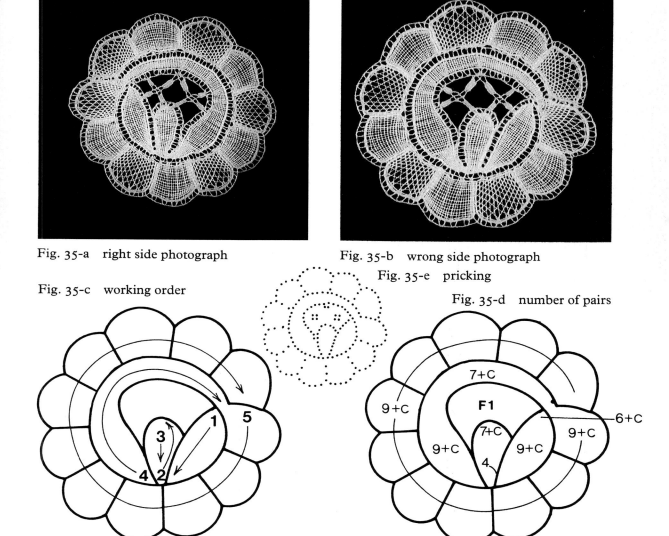

Fig. 35-a   right side photograph

Fig. 35-b   wrong side photograph

Fig. 35-c   working order

Fig. 35-e   pricking

Fig. 35-d   number of pairs

36 Grape

Fig. 36-a   right side photograph

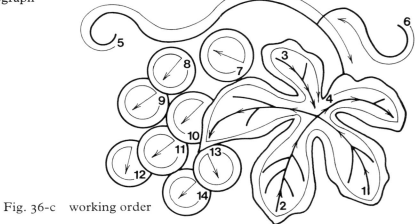

Fig. 36-c   working order

Fig. 36-b   wrong side photograph

8.5 = 8 pairs and a single thread
0.5 C = a single coarse thread

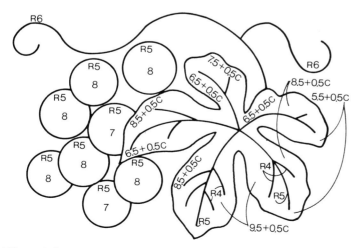

Fig. 36-d   number of pairs

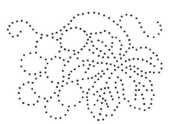

Fig. 36-e   pricking

37 Crane

Fig. 37-a   right side photograph

Fig. 37-c   working order

94

Fig. 37-b wrong
side photograph

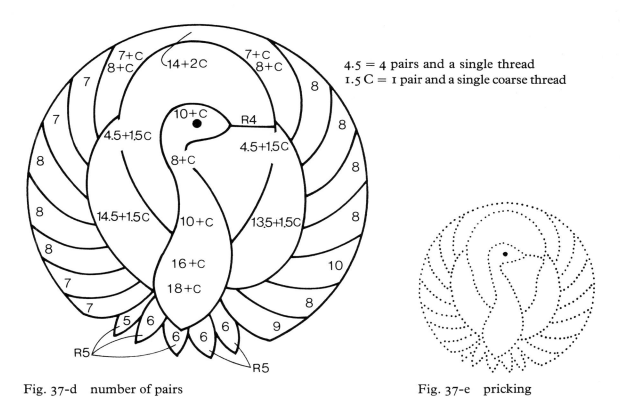

4.5 = 4 pairs and a single thread
1.5 C = 1 pair and a single coarse thread

Fig. 37-d number of pairs

Fig. 37-e pricking

95

38 Camellia

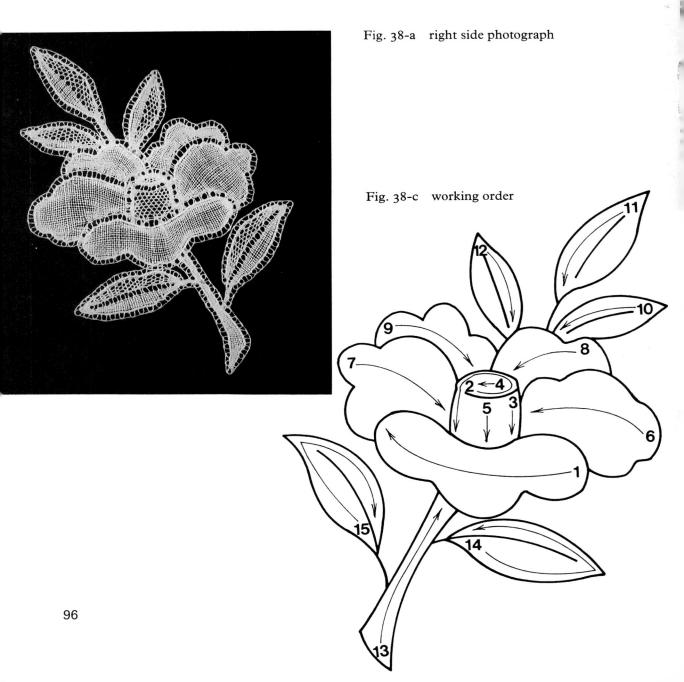

Fig. 38-a   right side photograph

Fig. 38-c   working order

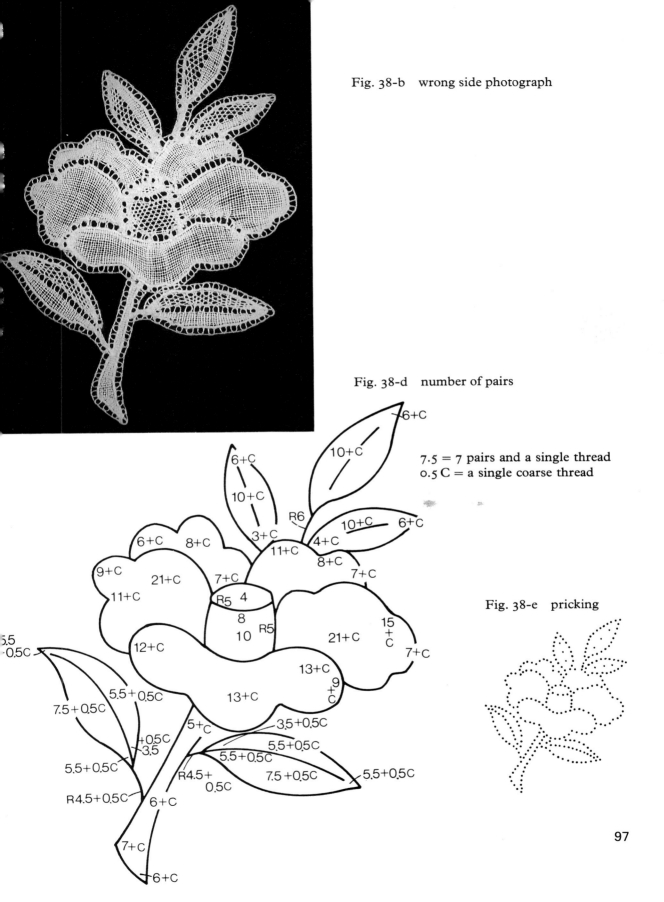

Fig. 38-b   wrong side photograph

Fig. 38-d   number of pairs

7.5 = 7 pairs and a single thread
0.5 C = a single coarse thread

Fig. 38-e   pricking

6+C

10+C

6+C

10+C

R6

10+C   6+C

3+C   4+C

11+C   8+C

7+C

6+C   8+C

9+C   7+C

21+C   R5   4

11+C   8   R5

10   15
+
C

12+C   21+C

13+C   7+C

5.5
0.5C

13+C   9
+
C

5.5+0.5C

7.5+0.5C   5+C   3.5+0.5C

5.5+0.5C

+0.5C
3.5   5.5+0.5C

5.5+0.5C   R4.5+   7.5+0.5C   5.5+0.5C
0.5C

R4.5+0.5C   6+C

7+C

6+C

39 Bonsai (pine tree)

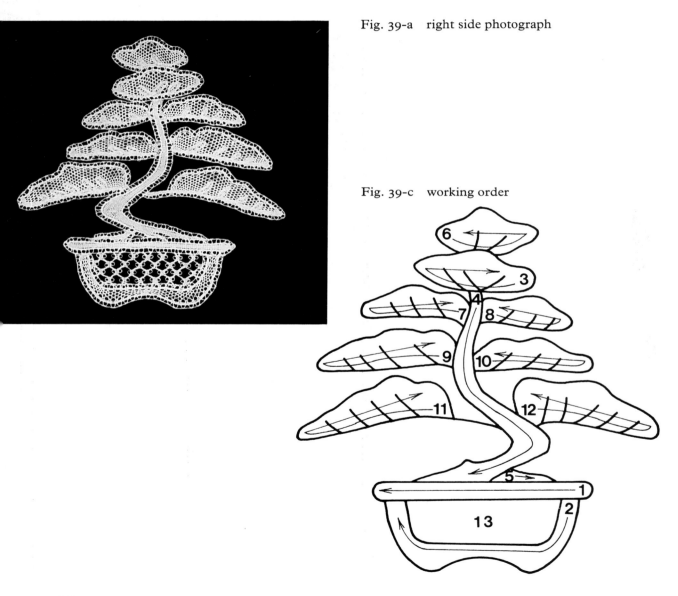

Fig. 39-a   right side photograph

Fig. 39-c   working order

Fig. 39-b   wrong side photograph

Fig. 39-d   number of pairs

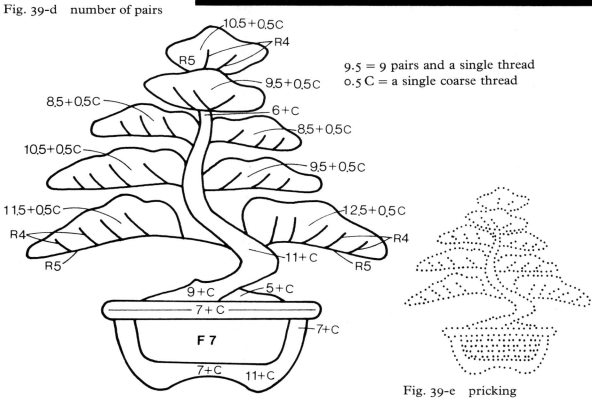

9.5 = 9 pairs and a single thread
0.5 C = a single coarse thread

10.5+0.5C
R4
R5
9.5+0.5C
8.5+0.5C
6+C
8.5+0.5C
10.5+0.5C
9.5+0.5C
11.5+0.5C
12.5+0.5C
R4
R4
R5
11+C
R5
9+C
5+C
7+C
7+C
F 7
7+C   11+C

Fig. 39-e   pricking

99

40 Peony

Fig. 40-a   right side photograph

Fig. 40-c   working order

Fig. 40-b   wrong side photograph

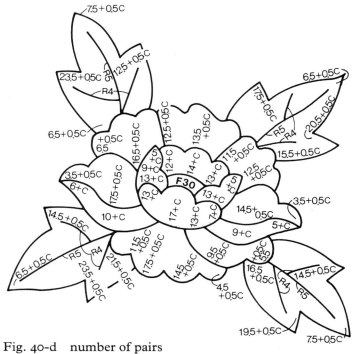

6.5 = 6 pairs and a single thread
0.5 C = a single coarse thread

Fig. 40-d   number of pairs

Fig. 40-f   right side photograph

Fig. 40-e   pricking

Appendix 1: Fillings

The great variety of fillings is one of the characteristic features of Honiton lace. Many Honiton lacemakers prick their fillings by eye, without the aid of graph paper, sometimes using a ruler as a guide. This makes it possible to fit a filling into a given shape in such a way that the groups of holes are complete at the edges and matching at both sides. An example of such filling worked into a curved space and a oval space can be seen in Pattern 1. However, to give the student some idea of the size the fillings should be, they are shown here on a grid and should be pricked on *one millimetre graph paper*.

The pairs for the fillings are sewn into the completed braid above and as near as possible to the groups of holes where they will be required, and often more than one pair will need to be sewn into the same hole. When sewing out pairs which have worked a row of filling, they are either tied three times and laid back to be cut off later, or they are brought in again to be used in a subsequent row if they are needed to fill in a widening space.

When a filling has been completed, and all the pairs have been sewn out and tied, the bobbins must be cut off and the ends of the thread trimmed before the pins are removed from the filling. Take out all the pins from the filling.

It often happens that the groups of holes of which many fillings consist are not complete at the edges of the space to be filled. When this happens, work the incomplete group as nearly as possible to the instructions given for these fillings – it is often possible to make a sewing into the edge of the braid to replace any missing holes. This can be clearly seen in Toad in the Hole (*filling 9*) in Estuary (*pattern 4*).

How to Prick

Transfer the dots for the chosen filling onto tracing paper, lay this over the pricking, and prick through into the space to be filled. Another method is to prick a block of the filling onto a piece of acetate, or used and washed X-ray plate; this is laid over the pricking and pricked through onto the pattern. These pricked 'templates' can be used again and again, providing that the pricking is done carefully, so as not to enlarge the holes in the template.

Filling 1   Diamond

Diagram 1

(Refer to diagram 1 and pattern 5: Blossom.) Sew in two pairs above A and two pairs above B. These may be sewn into adjacent pin holes of the completed braid. With the two pairs above A, work a whole stitch and twist both pairs three times. Add pin A between the two pairs. Repeat for hole B.

With each set of two pairs make a narrow leadwork to reach as far as C and D. When both leadworks are complete, twist all four pairs three times and set

103

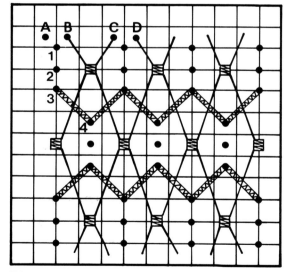

Grid pricking

pins C and D between each two pairs. With the two centre pairs work a whole stitch (No Pin). Twist both these pairs three times. With the two left-hand pairs work a whole stitch, twist both pairs three times and set pin E between them. With the two right-hand pairs work a whole stitch, twist both pairs three times and set pin F between them. With the two centre pairs work a whole stitch and twist both pairs three times (No Pin). Each two pairs now work another leadwork to the group of holes diagonally below, where they are joined by two pairs coming in from the opposite direction.

Filling 2   Toad in the Hole Variation

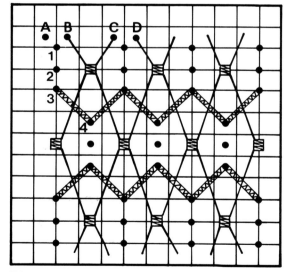

Diagram 2

(Refer to diagram 2 and pattern 6: Butterfly.) Sew two pairs into each hole A and D. Sew three pairs into each hole B and C. With the two pairs from A, work a bar of three half stitches to reach to I. Do the same with the two left-hand pairs from B. With the two middle pairs of these four, work a whole stitch and one twist and set pin I between them. Work a whole stitch and one twist with each two side pairs. Enclose the pin with a whole stitch and twist, using the two middle pairs. Set pin 2; then again work a whole stitch and twist with the two side pairs. Enclose the pin with the two middle pairs, making a whole stitch and twist. Set pin 3 and work another whole stitch and twist with each two side pairs. Enclose the pin with a whole stitch and twist.

Grid pricking

Work a bar of three half stitches with each two pairs and leave. Work another block of three holes as above, using the two pairs from D and the two right-hand pairs from C.

Twist the two pairs remaining at B and C five times each and make a square leadwork with them, twisting them five times again after the leadwork. Work the left-hand pair of the leadwork in whole stitch through the two nearest pairs coming from 3. Leave the leadwork pair aside and with the two pairs from 3 work a bar of three half stitches to reach to 4. Pass the right-hand leadwork pair through the nearest two pairs from the block made with the pairs from C and D. Leave the leadwork pair and work three half stitches with the other two pairs to reach to 4, where another block is made as above.

Filling 3   Jubilee

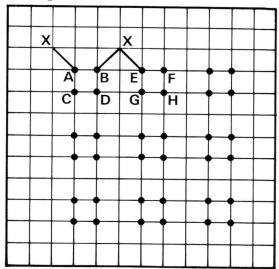

Diagram 3

Filling 4   No Pin

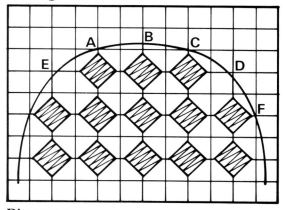

Diagram 4

(Refer to diagram 3 and pattern 9; Sampler.) Sew two pairs above A and two pairs above B. Work a whole stitch and three twists with the two left-hand pairs and set pin A between them. Work a whole stitch and three twists with the two right-hand pairs and set pin B between them. With the two middle pairs work a whole stitch and three twists (No Pin). With the two left-hand pairs work a whole stitch and three twists and set pin C between them. With the two right-hand pairs work a whole stitch and three twists and set pin D between them. With the two middle pairs work a whole stitch and three twists (No Pin). Enclose pins C and D with a whole stitch and three twists. Work the next group of four holes E, F, G and H as above. Work the two pairs from D through the two pairs from G in whole stitch. Twist all four pairs three times.

Each two pairs are now in position to work the next groups of four holes diagonally below, together with the two new pairs coming in from each side.

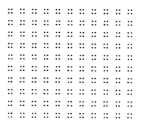

Grid picking

(Refer to diagram 4 and pattern 4: Estuary.) No pricking is needed for this filling, as the name suggests. It consists of rows of small square leadworks.

Sew one pair into each hole (or if the holes are very close together, into every other hole) in a straight line across the top of the space to be filled, and one pair on the right-hand side (at D on the diagram, usually the next hole slightly below C). Twist all pairs three times. Use the left-hand bobbin from D as the weaver for the first leadwork and take it under, over and back under the next two bobbins (from C).* It is now in the right position to weave the leadwork. When this has been completed, the weaver is again the second bobbin from the left. Twist both pairs three times. This brings the weaver to lie as the outer bobbin on the left. Leave the right-hand pair and work the next leadwork with the left-hand pair and the pair from B, *again using the same weaver,* which is first passed under, over and back under the two bobbins from B. Repeat from* across the row and after working the last leadwork, sew out the left-handpair (containing the runner, *see note 20d*) at E. If the shape being filled curves, as in the diagram sew in a new pair at D and one at F. Twist both pairs three times and work another row of leadworks. The pair sewn out at E may also be brought in again and twisted three times to make an extra leadwork if needed.

Filling 5 Snatch Bar with Leadworks

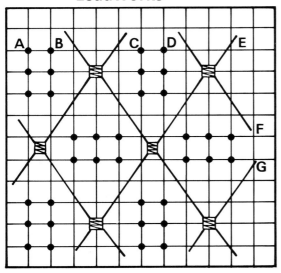

Diagram 5

(Refer to diagram 5.) Sew in two pairs above A and three pairs above B, C and D. If the six holes of the snatch bar are a little way away from the edge at which the pairs have been sewn in, work a whole stitch and one twist with the two pairs from A and the next two pairs from B, and use these four pairs to work the snatch bar as follows. Take the right-hand pair of the four as runners through the other three pairs in whole stitch, twist the runners seven times and set pin A under them. Take the runners back through three pairs, twist them seven times and set pin B under them. Continue working the runners back and forth, twisting round the pins, until all six holes have been used. After the last hole, work the runners back through three pairs, then twist the runners and the last pair they passed through once. Work a whole stitch and one twist with the other two pairs and leave. Work the next vertical snatch bar, using the two right-hand pairs

Grid pricking

from C and two left-hand pairs from D. Twist the two pairs remaining above B and C six times and use them to make a square leadwork. Twist the pairs six times again after the leadwork is completed and leave. The weaver in every leadwork must finish in the left-hand pair of the leadwork.

After completing the leadworks, lengthen the pairs that have made them so that they may be recognized subsequently. Work a similar leadwork with the pairs from above D and E. The right-hand pair of the leadwork is sewn out at F and brought in again. (This pair need not be lengthened.)

Sew in another new pair at F and three pairs at G. Four pairs now make a horizontal snatch bar in the same way as the vertical ones. The pairs of this snatch bar are now worked through the pairs of the snatch bar from CD with leadwork pairs between as follows. Take the left-hand pair of the FG snatch bar in whole stitch through the left-hand pair of the DE leadwork (this contains the weaver, so work carefully) and through the four parts of the CD snatch bar, and leave. Take the right-hand pair of the CD snatch bar through the DE leadwork pair and through the three remaining pairs of the FG snatch, and leave. ★ Take the first pair lying on the right of the DE leadwork pair through the leadwork pair and through three more pairs to the left and leave. Take the first pair lying on the left of the DE leadwork pair through the leadwork pair and through two more pairs to the right and leave.★ Take the right-hand pair from the BC leadwork in whole stitch through all nine pairs to the right and leave it to work the leadwork in the square below later. Take the first pair lying on the right of the DE leadwork pair through the DE leadwork and two more pairs, then leave. Take the first pair lying on the left of the DE leadwork through the DE leadwork and one more pair, then leave. Take the first pair lying on the right of the DE leadwork through the DE leadwork and one more pair, then leave. Take the first pair lying on the left of the DE leadwork through the DE leadwork. This finishes the crossing. Repeat from ★ to ★. This finishes the crossing.

The four pairs of the CD snatch are now in position to work the next snatch bar below them, but before this can be worked, make a whole stitch and one twist with each two pairs. Similarly, the pairs of the FG snatch bar will work the next horizontal snatch bar and the leadwork pair left in position to work the leadwork below this later, together with another pair coming from the left.

Filling 6　Four Pin

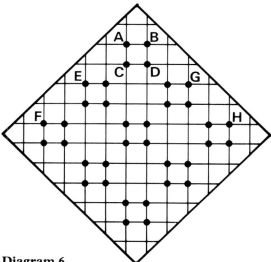

Diagram 6

(Refer to diagram 6 and pattern 1: Shell.) Sew in two pairs above each hole A, B, E, F, G and H. The four pairs from the above A and B work the first group of four holes as follows. ★ With the two left-hand pairs work a whole stitch, twist both pairs three times, and set pin A between them. With the two right-hand pairs work a whole stitch, twist both pairs three times and set pin B between them. With the two middle pairs work a whole stitch and twist both pairs three times (No Pin). With the two left-hand pairs work a whole stitch, twist both pairs three times and set pin C between them. With the two right-hand pairs work a whole stitch, twist both pairs three times and set pin D between them. With the two middle pairs work a whole stitch and twist both pairs three times (No Pin). ★ The two left hand pairs and the two pairs from above E now work the next group of four holes ★ to, ★, and at the end of the two left-hand pairs from this group meet the two pairs from above F to work the next group of four holes. Continue down this diagonal line until the row is complete; at the end, sew out the left-

hand two pairs. Return to the top and work the next group of holes with the two pairs from above G and the two pairs from D. Continue down this diagonal line, using the two left-hand pairs of each group with the pairs left from the previous line of four pins.

Filling 7　Whole Stitch Block Variation

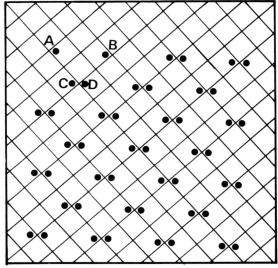

Diagram 7

(Refer to diagram 7 and pattern 7: Pride.) Four pairs are required to work each group of two holes. Sew in two pairs at A and B. Work a half stitch plait with each two pairs to reach to just above C and D. ★ Use the second pair from the right of these four pairs as runners and take them in whole stitch through two pairs to the left. Twist the runners seven times and set pin C under them. Work the runners through three pairs to the right, twist them seven times and set pin D under them. Work the runners through two pairs to the left and leave. With each two pairs work a half stitch plait to the group diagonally below (four half stitches should be enough), where they repeat the procedure from ★, together with two pairs coming from the other side.

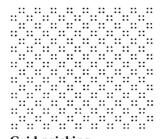

Grid pricking

Grid pricking

Filling 8   Blossom

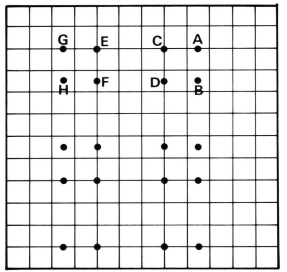

Diagram 8

(Refer to diagram 8.) Sew two pairs into the edge of the braid half-way between and above C and A. Sew in two pairs half-way between and to the right of A and B. Work a half stitch plait with each set of two pairs just to reach as far as the group of four holes. The four holes of each group are used to make purls as follows.

Use the right-hand pair of the left-hand plait to make a purle in hole A, ★ twisting this pair seven times using the right-hand bobbin to make the loop, and placing the pin under the right-hand thread, pointing to the left, twisting the point over the thread towards you and down into the hole. Lift the other thread round the pin from right to left. Twist the pair once. ★ Make a whole stitch with the two left-hand pairs and twist both pairs once. With the two centre pairs make a whole stitch and twist both pairs once. With the two right-hand pairs make a

whole stitch and use the right of these two pairs to make a purl in hole B ★ to ★.

Make a whole stitch with the two right-hand pairs. With the two left-hand pairs make a whole stitch and use the left of these pairs to make a purl in hole C, ★★ twisting this pair seven times. Place the pin under the left-hand bobbin, pointing towards the right. Twist the point over the thread towards you and down into the hole. Lift the other thread round the pin from left to right. Twist the pair twice (left over right). ★★ Work a whole stitch with the two left-hand pairs. Twist the two centre pairs once and make a whole stitch with them. Work a whole stitch with the two right-hand pairs. Use the left of these two pairs to make a purl at D, repeating ★★ to ★★. This completes one group of holes.

The two pairs between C and D now make a half stitch plait to reach as far as E, where they work the next group of four holes together with the two pairs sewn in above G and E. Put aside the two pairs between D and B. Continue along this row from right to left and after the last group of holes work a half stitch plait to reach the edge, where these two pairs are sewn out. With the two pairs put aside and left hanging below each group of holes, work half stitch plaits to reach the group of holes below. Sew two more pairs in on the right-hand side, and work a half stitch plait to the next set of holes.

Filling 9   Toad in the Hole

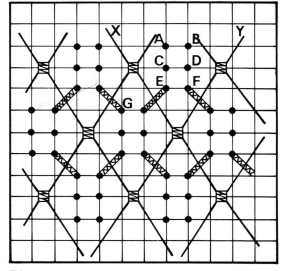

Diagram 9

```
::  ::  ::  ::  ::  ::  ::  ::  ::  ::
::  ::  ::  ::  ::  ::  ::  ::  ::  ::
::  ::  ::  ::  ::  ::  ::  ::  ::  ::
::  ::  ::  ::  ::  ::  ::  ::  ::  ::
::  ::  ::  ::  ::  ::  ::  ::  ::  ::
::  ::  ::  ::  ::  ::  ::  ::  ::  ::
::  ::  ::  ::  ::  ::  ::  ::  ::  ::
::  ::  ::  ::  ::  ::  ::  ::  ::  ::
::  ::  ::  ::  ::  ::  ::  ::  ::  ::
::  ::  ::  ::  ::  ::  ::  ::  ::  ::
```

Grid pricking

(Refer to diagram 9 and pattern 4: Estuary.) Sew in one pair above X and Y and three pairs each above A and B. The pair from X and the left-hand pair from A are each twisted five times and used to make a square leadwork after which they are twisted five times again and left. The right-hand pair from B and the pair from Y are left to work a similar leadwork in the next row. With the two pairs from above A work a whole stitch and one twist. Do the same with the two pairs from above B.

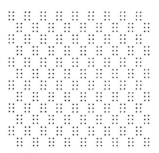

Grid pricking

To work the group of six holes, or 'snatch' (as it is called in Devon) use the right-hand pair of these four as runners, and work them through three pairs to the left in whole stitch. Twist the runners seven times, set pin A under them and continue working the runners back and forth to B, C, D, E and F, twisting seven times round each pin. After F has been set, work back through three pairs, twist the runners and the last pair they passed through once and leave them. Work a whole stitch and one twist with the other two pairs and leave. This completes the snatch.

The right-hand pair of the leadwork now works through the two left-hand pairs of the snatch in whole stitch, and is now left for a leadwork in the next row. With the two pairs from the snatch through which the leadwork pair has passed, work a whole stitch and one twist. The right-hand pair of these two becomes the runner pair for the next snatch. This is worked with these two pairs and two more coming in from the other side, either from another snatch or sewn in at the side of the space. The snatch is begun by working the runners through three pairs to the left, twisting them seven times and setting pin G under them. The other two pairs from the first snatch are left to work a snatch in the next row, after a leadwork pair has passed through them. It is best to work this filling in diagonal rows from top right to bottom left.

Filling 10 Italian

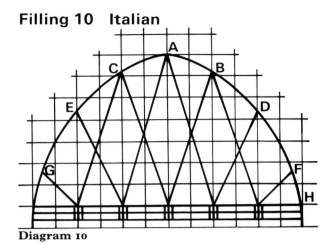

Diagram 10

(Refer to diagram 10.) This is worked without a pricking. Sew in pairs as indicated in the diagram. The pairs across the top are sewn in at every hole, or if the holes are very close together at every other hole. Make a whole stitch and three twists with each two pairs from A, B and C. With the right-hand pair from A and the left-hand pair from B work a whole stitch and three twists. With the left-hand pair from A and the right-hand pair from C work a whole stitch and three twists. Twist the pair from D three times and use it with the right-hand pair from B to work a whole stitch and three twists. Twist the pair from E three times and use it with the left-hand pair from C to work a whole stitch and three twists. Twist the pair from F three times and use it with the next pair on the left to work a whole stitch. Do not twist. Work a whole stitch with the next two pairs on the left; leave these, work another whole stitch with the next two pairs on the left, and so on across the row. The odd pair at the end is joined by the pair from G which has first been twisted three times.

There are now complete sets of four bobbins across the row and complete diamonds have been formed above these. The pair sewn in at H now becomes the runner pair for the horizontal rows dividing the diamonds. Twist this pair three times, * work it in whole stitch through the next set of two pairs, twist the runners three times and repeat from * across the row, sewing the runner pair into the braid at the other side, after pulling it up well. Ensure the line is horizontal and the pairs through which the runners pass are not twisted.

After sewing, tie the runners once, twist them three times and work a return row as above, again sewing the runners in at the right-hand side into hole H. Occasionally, if the first line is not quite straight, the second sewing may be made into the next hole below H. Again, twist the runners three times and work another row as the first, sewing them out at the end and into the same hole as the first sewing on that side. This completes one repeat of the pattern. The runners may be needed for the twisted diamond work, otherwise they are tied three times and laid back to be cut off later.

The next set of diamonds is worked as above and is started by working a whole stitch and three twists with each set of four bobbins hanging below the last horizontal bar. The diamond work at the sides will vary according to the shape of the space; the odd pairs at the sides will either be sewn in at the sides, twisted three times, and brought back again to work with any odd pairs, or an extra pair may need to be sewn in, to use with the odd pair at the sides to form extra diamonds in a widening space. There must be complete sets of four bobbins ready before the horizontal line is worked.

Filling 11   Swing and a Pin

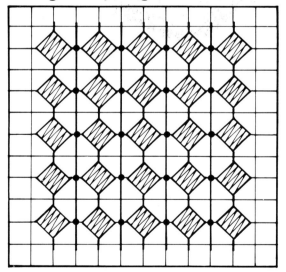

Diagram 11

(Refer to diagram 11 and pattern 7: Brooch pattern.) The holes needed for this filling are pricked in as the filling progresses. The first row consists of leadworks, which are sewn in and made in exactly the same way as described for No Pin (*filling 4*).

The rows of leadworks alternate with rows in which a twisted pair is worked through the leadwork pairs and pinholes are made, as follows. Sew in one

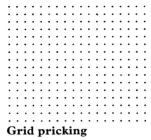

Grid pricking

pair at the right-hand edge immediately below the level of the leadworks. Twist this pair three times and work a whole stitch with the pair from the nearest leadwork. Twist both pairs three times. ★ Prick a hole immediately below the leadwork and set a pin into it between these two pairs. Enclose the pin with a whole stitch and three twists. Leave the right-hand pair, and with the left-hand pair and the next pair on the left, work a whole stitch and three twists. Repeat from ★ across the row. Ensure that the pinholes are pricked in a straight line. Sew out the left-hand pairs at the left side. The next row is a leadwork row.

Filling 12   Pin and a Stitch

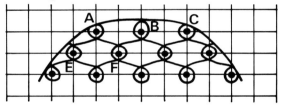

Diagram 12

(Refer to diagram 12 and pattern 3: Maze.) Sew in two pairs above each hole along the top line. With each two pairs, work a whole stitch and three twists and set pins between them, enclosing the pins with a whole stitch and three twists. The pairs now divide to work the holes diagonally below them, the right-hand pair from A and the left-hand pair from B working hole F, etc., as above. The left-hand pair from A meets a new pair sewn in at the edge and twisted three times, to work hole E.

Grid pricking

Filling 13   Pin and a Chain

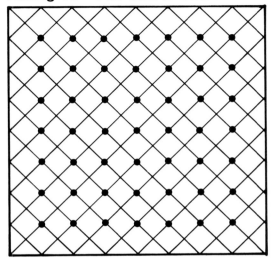

Diagram 13

(Refer to diagram 13.) This consists of a pinhole row and a row made with a twisted pair alternating. Sew in two pairs above each hole along the top. With each two pairs work a whole stitch, twist both pairs three times, set a pin between them and enclose the pin with a whole stitch. Do not twist. This completes the first horizontal row of holes.

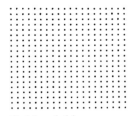

Grid pricking

Sew in a new pair at the right-hand side, between the row of holes just worked and the next row. Twist this pair three times, and use it as a runner pair to work in whole stitch through the two pairs which enclosed the nearest pin. ★ Twist the runners three times and work them through the next two pairs in whole stitch, repeat from ★ across the row and sew out the runners at the end after twisting them three times and pulling up well. The next row is a pinhole row and is worked like the first.

Filling 14   Swing and a Stitch

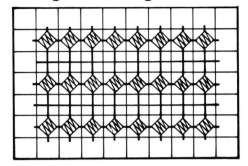

Diagram 14

(Refer to diagram 14 and pattern 3: Maze.) This filling needs no pricking and is similar to Swing and a Pin (*filling 11*). It consists of rows of leadworks and rows made with a twisted pair alternating. Work the first row of leadworks as explained in No Pin (*filling 4*). Sew in a new pair at the right-hand edge immediately below the level of the leadworks. Twist this pair three times and work a whole stitch with the nearest leadwork pair, ★ twist both pairs three times, leave the right-hand pair and, with the left-hand pair and the next leadwork pair, work a whole stitch. Repeat from ★ across the row and sew out the left-hand pair at the end of the row, after pulling it as much as possible into a straight line below the leadworks.

Filling 15   Trolly Net

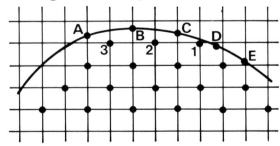

Diagram 15

(Refer to diagram 15 and pattern 18: Reed design.) This filling is worked in horizontal rows. (Prick diagonally for a smaller mesh.) Sew in one pair at A, B and C above and between each two holes of

Grid pricking

the filling. Sew in one pair at D on the right-hand side level with the first row of holes. Twist all pairs two or three times, according to the distance between the pinholes and the edge of the braid. With the pairs from D and C work a half stitch, twist both pairs four times and set pin 1 between them. ★ Leave the right-hand pair, and with the left-hand pair and the pair from B work another half stitch and four twists. Set a pin between these pairs. Repeat from ★ across the row, using the next pair on the left for each stitch. Sew out the left-hand pair at the end of the row. Sew in a new pair at E, twist it and use it with the pair from 1 to work a half stitch and four twists. Set a pin between these pairs. Repeat from ★ above. The threads run in a diagonal line from top left to bottom right.

Filling 16   Spotted Net

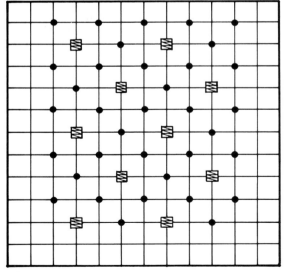

Diagram 16

(Refer to diagram 16 and pattern 9: Sampler.) Work the first row as above. In the next row leadworks alternate with net stitches. The leadworks take the place of one pinhole and are made with the pairs which would normally have made this pinhole. The position of the leadworks may be marked on the pricking before beginning work. The weaver for the

Grid pricking

leadwork is the second bobbin from the right of the four threads, and it is passed under the next thread on the left, and over and back under the next thread, to bring it into the correct position to begin weaving. After the leadwork is finished, twist both pairs three times, so that the weaver becomes the last thread on the left of the four, and remains the leading thread and weaver for the whole row. The next row is a net row, and in the following row the leadworks come in alternate spaces to the last leadwork row.

Filling 17   Cartwheel

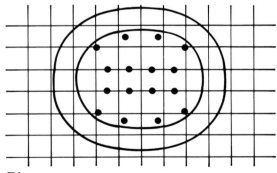

Diagram 17

(Refer to diagram 17 and pattern 5: Blossom.) This is often used as a filling for a flower or for a round or oval space. It can be made with six, eight or ten leadworks. Sew two pairs for each leadwork into two adjacent braid holes above the single holes at the top of the filling. With each two pairs make a whole stitch, twist both pairs three times and set

:::

::::

:::::

Grid pricing

pins between them. With each two pairs, work a narrow leadwork to the middle row of holes. Twist all pairs three times and set pins between each two pairs into the top row of the holes in the middle. ★ Leave the outside pair on each side and join all other adjoining pairs with a whole stitch and three twists. ★ Laying each pair with its original partner (i.e. bringing in the two outer pairs), work a whole stitch and three twists with each two pairs, and set pins between each two pairs into the lower row of holes in the middle. Repeat from ★ to ★. Work a leadwork with each two pairs to the holes at the lower edge, twist each pair three times, set pins between them and work a whole stitch. Make three twists if the holes are a little distance from the braid, and sew out.

Filling 18   Purl Pin Bars

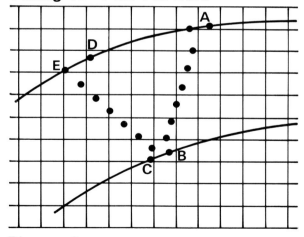

Diagram 18

(Refer to diagram 18 and pattern 3: Maze.) These are made with four pairs which are sewn into two adjacent holes at A. With the first pair on the right, work through the other three pairs to the left, twist the runners once and leave them. ★ Use the last pair

Grid pricking

of runners worked through as new runners to work through two pairs to the right. Use this pair to make a purl on the right side of the bar, twisting it seven times, placing a pin under the outer thread, pointing towards the left, and twisting the pin over the thread towards you and down into the first pinhole. Twist the second thread up round the pin from right to left and pull up. Twist the pair once and work back with this pair through three pairs to the left, twist the runners once and leave them. Repeat from ★.

When the bar has reached the opposite braid and the last purl has been made, work the runners back to the left and through to the purl edge again and sew them to the braid at B. Work one whole stitch with the sewn pair and the next pair on the left, leave the left of these two pairs, and sew the right-hand pair at C. Tie this pair once, and use it as the runner to work the next bar. When the last purl of the second bar has been made, work the runners to the plain side and sew them at D. Work a whole stitch with the sewn pair and the next pair on the right, leave the right of these pairs and sew the left pair at E. The purls are usually made on the right side of each bar, but they may be worked on the left, or the left and right on alternate bars.

Filling 19   Brick

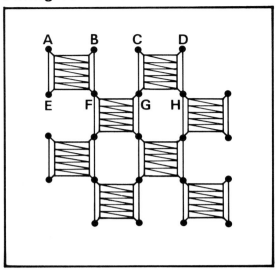

Diagram 19

(Refer to diagram 19 and pattern 9: Sampler.) Sew two pairs above each hole across the top of the pattern. With each two pairs, make a whole stitch and twist both pairs three times. Set a pin between each two pairs in the holes below them, and enclose the pin with a whole stitch and three twists. With the right-hand pair from A and the left-hand pair from B, make a leadwork. Repeat with the right-hand pair from C and the left-hand pair from D. Twist all the leadwork pairs three times. With the pair hanging from A and the nearest leadwork pair * make a whole stitch, twist both pairs three times, set pin E between them and enclose the pin with a whole stitch and three twists *. Repeat from * to * across the row with each two pairs (pins F, G, H, etc.). In the next row leadworks are made in alternate spaces (e.g. the right-hand pair from F and the left-hand pair from G make a leadwork) and at the end, the leadwork pairs are joined to the pairs hanging on either side, and the next row of pins is set as above.

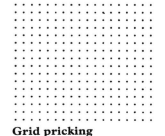

Grid pricking

Filling 20   Rib Squares and Leadwork

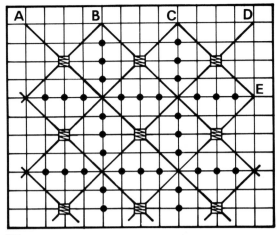

Diagram 20

(Refer to diagram 20 and pattern 9: Sampler.) Sew in a pair at A and at D. Sew in six pairs (three into each of two adjacent holes at B and six pairs at C. Sew in four pairs (two into each of two adjacent holes) at E. With the right outer pair from C and the pair from D, each twisted five times, work a square leadwork. Twist the pairs five times again and leave. Work similar leadwork with the left outer pair from C and the right outer pair from B. With the four pairs left at C work a rib (*note 18*) with the pinholes on the right, down the three holes below C. Leave. Work the right-hand pair from CD leadwork in whole stitch through the four pairs from E and leave it to work a leadwork in the space below later. With the four pairs from E work the three horizontal holes in rib with the pinholes on the right.

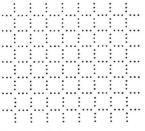

Grid pricking

The pairs from the vertical and horizontal ribs are now crossed, together with two leadwork pairs as follows. Lengthen the two threads of the left-hand pair of the CD leadwork (this contains the weaver so be careful not to draw up the leadwork) and lay this pair over the four pairs of the vertical rib from C. Now lift the four pairs of the horizontal rib completely over the other five pairs. The four pairs of the rib from E are now on the left, then comes the leadwork pair and the four pairs of the rib from C are on the right. Now take the right-hand pair from the BC leadwork in whole stitch through the nine crossed pairs, pull up this pair and the crossed pairs well and leave. Leave the leadwork pair on the right to use later for the leadwork, together with the pair from E. This completes one repeat of the pattern.

Begin the next repeat by working the leadwork with the pair from A and the outer left-hand pair from B. Then the three vertical holes of rib from B and the three horizontal holes of the rib with the four left-hand pairs of those from the last crossing. In these instructions the ribs have been worked with the pinholes on the right of each rib, but they may equally well be made on the left. They should always be made on the same side throughout a filling.

Filling 21   Straight Pin

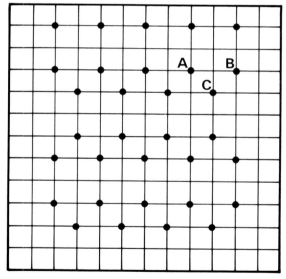

Diagram 21

(Refer to diagram 21 and pattern 9. Sampler.) Sew two pairs above each hole across the top of the pattern; with each two pairs make a whole stitch, twist both pairs three times and set pins into the holes between them. With each two pairs work a narrow leadwork to reach the pinholes in the next

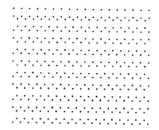

Grid pricking

row. Twist the pairs three times and set a pin between the pairs of each leadwork. Enclose the pins with a whole stitch and twist both pairs three times. The right-hand pair from A and the left-hand pair from B now meet and repeat the pattern (i.e. make a whole stitch and three twists, set pin C between them and use them to make another leadwork). The remaining pairs from A and B meet a pair coming from each side.

Filling 22   Whole Stitch Block

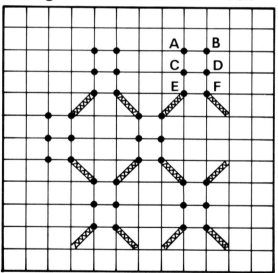

Diagram 22

(Refer to diagram 22.) The blocks or 'snatches' are worked as in Toad in the Hole (*filling 9*). Four pairs are sewn in above each snatch hole and a whole stitch and one twist is made with each two pairs before beginning to work the snatch. After the last pin of the snatch has been set, work the runners through to the outer side once more, twist them and the last pair they passed through once and leave

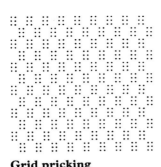

Grid pricking

them. The other two pairs make a whole stitch and twist once. The right-hand pair of the two from E becomes the runner pair for the next snatch diagonally below and works through three pairs to the left, then twists round pin G.

Filling 23 Four Pin and Leadwork

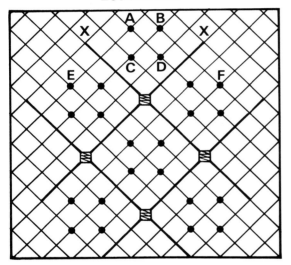

Diagram 23

(Refer to diagram 23 and pattern 28: Oriental flower.) Sew in two pairs above each hole A, B, E and F and one pair at each point X. Using the four pairs above A and B, work the first group of four holes as follows. * With the two left-hand pairs work a whole stitch, twist both pairs three times and set pin A between them. With the two right-hand pairs work a whole stitch, twist both pairs three times and set pin B between them. With the two middle pairs work a whole stitch and twist both pairs three times (No Pin). With the two left-hand pairs work a whole

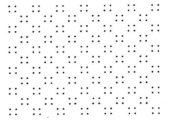

Grid pricking

stitch, twist both pairs three times and set pin C between them. With the two right-hand pairs work a whole stitch, twist both pairs three times and set pin D between them. With the two middle pairs work a whole stitch and twist both pairs three times (No Pin). * Now enclose pins C and D with a whole stitch. Twist the pairs from X three times and work them in whole stitch through the pairs from C and D, so that they meet in the space below the first group of holes, where they are twisted three times and work a square leadwork. Twist both pairs three times after the leadwork and leave them. The pairs from C and E work the next four pin group from * to *, after which the two lower pairs are enclosed with a whole stitch, and the left-hand pair of the leadwork is worked in whole stitch through the two right-hand pairs of this group.

Filling 24 Toad in the Hole with Wide Leadwork

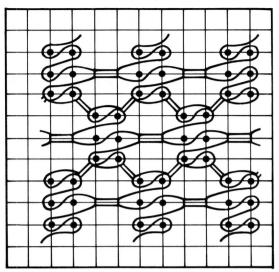

Diagram 24

(Refer to diagram 24.) This is similar to Toad in the Hole (*filling 9*), but the leadwork pairs are omitted, the leadwork being made with the runners from adjacent snatches half way through the snatch. Work horizontally as follows. Four pairs are sewn in above each whole stitch block or snatch and a whole stitch and twist is made with each two pairs before beginning the snatch. The runners are the right-hand pair of each set of four and they work back and forth through the other three, as shown in the diagram, seven twists being made round each pin, except the middle pins. When the middle pin in each of the two adjacent snatches has been set, the runner pairs are twisted three times and meet to make a wide, shallow leadwork, after which they are twisted three times again, and each continues to weave its own snatch.

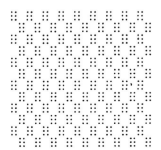

Grid pricking

Filling 25 Four Pin with Half Stitch Bars

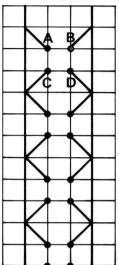

Diagram 25

(Refer to diagram 25 and pattern 3: Maze.) This is used to fill a long narrow space, being composed of groups of four pins, the pairs being attached to the edges of the braid between groups of holes. Sew two pairs into the braid on each side, diagonally above the group of four holes, then work a half stitch plait with each set of two to form a bar to reach the group of holes. * The last stitch of the bar should be a whole stitch, each pair being twisted three times before pins A and B are set between them. With the two middle pairs, work a whole stitch and three

Grid pricking

twists (No Pin). With the two left-hand pairs, work a whole stitch and three twists, and set pin C between them. With the two right-hand pairs, work a whole stitch and three twists, and set pin D between them. With the two middle pairs, work a whole stitch and three twists (No Pin). Each two pairs now work a half stitch bar to reach to the edges of the braid half way between the sets of holes, where they are sewn, tied once (to hold the bar firm), and then used to work a bar to the next set of holes. Repeat from *.

117

Filling 26 Devonshire Cutwork (Swing and a Stitch Variation)

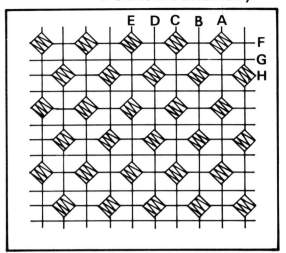

Diagram 26

(Refer to diagram 26.) No pricking is needed. Sew in one pair at every hole or, if the holes are close together, at every other hole, across the top of the space, and one pair on the right side at F, one hole below A. Twist all pairs three times. The left-hand bobbin of the pair from F is the weaver for the leadwork. * It is taken under the next thread on the left and over and back under the next thread, to bring it into the right position to begin weaving a small square leadwork. When this is finished and both pairs have been twisted three times, the weaver is the outer thread on the left of these four. Leave the right-hand pair and with the left-hand pair and the pair from B work a whole stitch and three twists. Pull up the stitch carefully. Leave the right-hand pair and with the left-hand pair and the pair from C make another leadwork, using the same weaver as for the previous leadwork. This is the second thread from the right of these four. Repeat from * across the row, sewing in the pair which has woven across at the end. For the next row a new pair is sewn in at G, and this is twisted three times. Work a whole stitch and three twists (both pairs) with each pair across the row, after which it is pulled up carefully into a straight line and sewn out on the other side. In the following row the leadworks are made with the pair which made a stitch in the first row, so that they come in alternate spaces and a new space is sewn in at H to work this row.

Filling 27 Devonshire Cutwork Variation

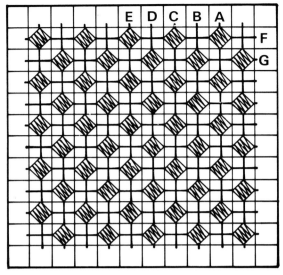

Diagram 27

(Refer to diagram 27.) No pricking is needed. Sew in one pair at every hole or, if the holes are close together, at every other hole, across the top of the space, and one pair on the right side at F, one hole below A. Twist all pairs three times. The left-hand bobbin of the pair from F is the weaver for the leadwork. * It is taken under the next thread on the left and over and back under the next thread, to bring it into the right position to begin weaving a small square leadwork. When this is finished and both pairs have been twisted three times, the weaver is the outer thread on the left of these four. Leave the right-hand pair and with the left-hand pair and the pair from B, work a whole stitch and three twists. Pull up the stitch carefully. Leave the right-hand pair and with the left-hand pair and one pair from C make another leadwork, using the same weaver as for the previous leadwork; this is the second thread from the right of these four. Repeat from * across the row, sewing in the pair which has woven across at the end. For the next row a new pair is sewn in at G, and in this row the leadworks are made with the pair that made the whole stitch, so that they come in alternate spaces, with a whole stitch made between the leadworks. Repeat these two rows to fill the space.

Filling 28   Brick Variation

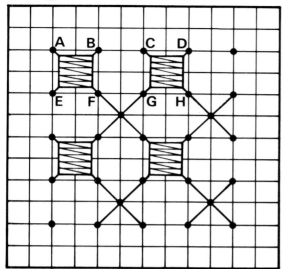

Diagram 28

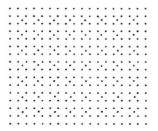

Grid pricking

leadwork pair * make a whole stitch, twist both pairs three times, set pin E between them and enclose the pin with a whole stitch and three twists *. Repeat from * to * across the row with each two pairs (pins F, G, H, I etc.). In the next row work the two pairs from F through the two pairs from G in whole stitch. Twist each pair three times. Repeat with pairs from H and I. These two rows are repeated until the space is filled.

Filling 29   Leadwork Bars

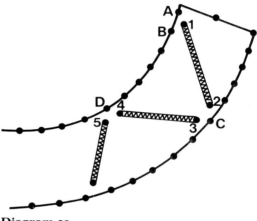

Diagram 29

(Refer to diagram 28.) Sew two pairs above each hole across the top of the pattern. With each two pairs make a whole stitch and twist both pairs three times. Set a pin between each two pairs in the holes below them, and enclose the pin with a whole stitch and three twists. With the right-hand pair from A and the left-hand pair from B, make a leadwork. Repeat with the right-hand pair from C and the left-hand pair from D. Twist all the leadwork pairs three times. With the pair hanging from A and the nearest

(Refer to diagram 29 and pattern 1: Shell.) Sew a pair into the braid at pinholes A and B. Make a whole stitch and twist each pair three times. Put a pin into the single pinhole 1. Work a leadwork towards pinhole C. Twist the pairs three times. Set a pin in hole 2, make a whole stitch, and twist each pair three times on the pin. Sew the outer pair into pinhole C, tie once, make a whole stitch, twist three times and put a pin into hole 3. Make the leadwork from hole 3 to hole 4 and repeat from 4 to 5 as from 2 to 3, until the last pinhole is reached. At the last pinhole, twist each pair three times and put a pin in the single pinhole; make a whole stitch, twist each pair three times and sew out each pair into the nearest two holes of the braid.

Filling 30 Swing Leadworks

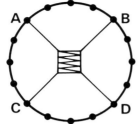

Diagram 30

(Refer to diagram 30 and pattern 2: Forget-me-not.) Sew on pair at holes A and B and tie each pair once. Twist each pair three times – (depending upon the size of the space to be filled, more twists may be necessary so that the single leadwork will lie in the central position). Work a small square leadwork. Twist the pairs three times and sew out at C and D, taking care not to pull the weaver thread. Tie each pair three times. These Swing Leadworks are only suitable to fill small spaces.

Filling 31 Blossom Variation

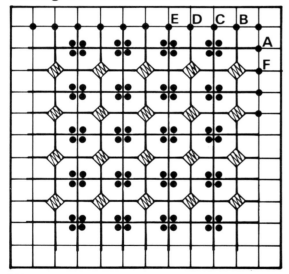

Diagram 31

(Refer to diagram 31.) The pricking is the same as for Blossom filling (*filling 8*), and the four holes are worked as instructed in filling 8. Sew two pairs at A, C and E for the blossom. Sew one pair at B, D and F to work the row after the blossom and between each blossom. Twist the pair from B five times and use the two pairs from A to work three half stitches of the plait. These two pairs then work through the single pair from B in whole stitch. Work three more half stitches to complete the plait between the blossom holes. Continue along this row working the blossom and through the single pair from E as above. The row will end with a plait and be sewn out. Return and work from right to left for each row. Twist the pairs from F and B five times; use these two pairs to make a leadwork (twist each pair five times after the leadwork has been made). Leave the

:: :: :: :: :: :: :: :: :: ::
:: :: :: :: :: :: :: :: :: ::
:: :: :: :: :: :: :: :: :: ::
:: :: :: :: :: :: :: :: :: ::
:: :: :: :: :: :: :: :: :: ::
:: :: :: :: :: :: :: :: :: ::
:: :: :: :: :: :: :: :: :: ::
:: :: :: :: :: :: :: :: :: ::
:: :: :: :: :: :: :: :: :: ::

Grid pricking

pair on the right and use the left of the two pairs, which should contain the runner, to work in whole stitch through the two pairs of the blossom above. These two pairs should have three half stitches of the plait made before working through and three more will be made after working through to reach the four holes of the blossom below. Continue this row, working a leadwork with the pair from D (five twists before and after the leadwork) alternating the whole stitch through two pairs of the blossom and a leadwork made with the single pair between each blossom.

Filling 32   Cushion

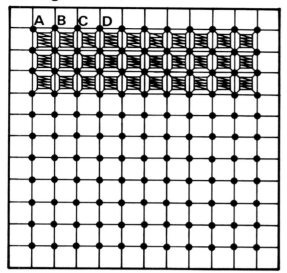

Diagram 32

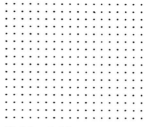

Grid pricking

(Refer to diagram 32.) This filling consists of rows of leadworks and pinholes. Sew two pairs at each of the top pinholes A, B, C and D. With each two pairs make a whole stitch and one twist, enclose the pin with a whole stitch and one twist. Take the right pair from A and the left pair from B to make a leadwork down to the next row of holes and leave. Next, make a leadwork with the right pair from B and the left from C. With one pair from B and the left from C make a whole stitch and twist once; put a pin in the hole below B, enclose with a whole stitch and one twist, then leave. Make a leadwork with the pairs from C and D. Continue likewise to the end of the row. If there is no space for a leadwork here, the odd pair will be sewn out; otherwise one extra pair will need to be sewn into the braid to work out this last leadwork.

Appendix II: Lace suppliers

United Kingdom

Alby Lace Museum
Cromer Road
Alby
Norfolk
NR11 7QE

E. Braggins and Sons
26–36 Silver Street
Bedford

Chrisken Bobbins
26 Cedar Drive
Kingsclere
Newbury
Bucks
RG15 8TD

T. Brown
Temple Lane Cottage
Littledean
Cinderford
Gloucestershire
GL14 3NX

Stephen Cook
'Cottage Crafts'
6 Woodland Close
Flackwell Heath
Buckinghamshire
HP10 9EP

Leonie Cox
The Old School
Childswickham
Near Broadway
Worcs
WR12 7HD

J. and J. Ford
October Hill
Upper Way
Upper Longdon
Rugeley
Staffordshire
WS15 1QB

Frank Herring & Sons
27 High Street
Dorchester
Dorset
DT1 1UP

Honiton Lace Shop
44 High Street
Honiton
Devon

D. J. Hornsby
149 High Street
Burton Latimer
Kettering
Northants
NN15 5RL

All branches of John Lewis

Lambourn Valley Cottage Industries
11 Oxford Street
Lambourn
Berks
RG16 7XS

Mace and Nairn
89 Crane Street
Salisbury
Wiltshire
SP1 2PY

Appendix II: Lace suppliers

The Needlewoman
21 Needless Abbey
off New Street
Birmingham

Newnham Lace Equipment
15 Marlowe Close
Basingstoke
Hants
RG24 9DD

T. Parker
124 Corhampton Road
Boscombe East
Bournemouth
BH6 5NZ

Dorothy Pearce
5 Fulshaw Avenue
Wilmslow
Cheshire

Bryn Phillips
'Pantglas'
Cellan
Lampeter
SA48 8JD

Jack Piper
'Silverlea'
Flax Lane
Glemsford
Suffolk
CO10 7RS

Hilary Rickets
4 Island Cottages
Mapledurwell
Basingstoke
Hants
RG25 2LU

The Royal School of Needlework
5 King Street
Covent Garden
London
WC2 8HN

Peter and Beverley Scarlett
Strupak
Hill Head
Coldwells
Ellon
Grampian

J. S. Sear
Lacecraft Supplies
8 Hill View
Sherrington
Buckinghamshire

Sebalace
Waterloo Mills
Howden Road
Silsden
W. Yorks

A. Sells
49 Pedley Lane
Clifton
Shefford
Bedfordshire

D. H. Shaw
47 Zamor Crescent
Thurscroft
Rotherham
S. Yorks
S66 9QD

Shireburn Lace
Finkle Court
Finkle Hill
Sherburn in Elmet
N. Yorks
LS25 6EB

Sizelands
1 Highfield Road
Winslow
Bucks

Stephen Simpson
Avenham Road Works
Preston
Lancs

S.M.P.
4 Garners Close
Chalfont St Peter
Bucks
SL9 0HB

Christine and David Springett
21 Hillmorton Road
Rugby
Warwickshire
CV22 5DF

Valley House Crafts Studios
Ruston
Scarborough
N. Yorks

George White
Delaheys Cottage
Thistle Hill
Knaresborough
N. Yorks
HG5 8LS

Christopher Williams
19 Morison Avenue
Parkstone
Poole
Dorset
BH12 4AD

Bobbin Makers

T. Brown
Temple Lane Cottage
Littledean
Cinderford
Gloucestershire

T. Parker
124 Corhampton Road
Boscombe East
Bournemouth
BH6 5NZ

Richard Viney
Unit 7
Port Royal Street
Southsea
Hants
PO5 4NP

George White
Delaheys Cottage
Thistle Hill
Knaresborough
N. Yorks.

Silk embroidery and lace thread

E. and J. Piper
Silverlea
Flax Lane
Glemsford
Suffolk
CO10 7RS

Silk Weaving Yarn

Hilary Chetwynd
Kipping Cottage
Cheriton
Alresford
Hants
SO24 0PW

Frames and Mounts

Doreen Campbell
'Highcliff'
Bremilham Road
Malmesbury
Wilts

Matt Coloured Transparent Adhesive Film

Heffers
26 King Street
Cambridge
CB1 1LN

United States of America

Berga Ullman Inc.
P.O. Box 918
North Adams
Massachusetts
01247

Frederick J. Fawcett
129 South Street
Boston
Massachusetts
02130

Frivolité
15526 Densmore N.
Seattle
Washington
98113

Happy Hands
3007 S. W. Marshall
Pendleton
Oregon
97180

Appendix II: Lace suppliers

Lacis
2990 Adline Street
Berkeley
California
94703

Robin's Bobbins
RTL Box 1736
Mineral Bluff
Georgia
30559

Robin and Russ Handweavers
533 North Adams Street
McMinnvills
Oregon
97128

Some Place
2990 Adline Street
Berkeley
California
94703

Osma G. Todd Studio
319 Mendoza Avenue
Coral Gables
Florida
33134

The Unique And Art Lace Cleaners
5926 Delman Boulevard
St Louis
Missouri
63112

Van Scriver Bobbin Lace
130 Cascadilla Park
Ithaca
New York
14850

Australia

Tulis Crafts
201 Avoca Street
Randwick, NSW 2031

Spindle and Loom
Arcade 83
Longueville Road
Lane Cove, NSW 2066

The Lacemaker
94 Fordham Avenue
Hartwell
Victoria 3124

Dentelles Lace Supplies
3 Narrak Close
Jindalee
Queensland 4074

Belgium

Kantcentrum
Balstraat 14
8000 Bruges

Manufacture Belge de Dentelle
6 Galerie de la Reine
Galeriers Royales St Hubert
1000 Bruxelles

France

La Dentelle
2 Rue Duguesclin
43000 Le Puy en Velay

Rougier and Plé
13-15 bd des Filles du Calvaire
75003 Paris

Holland

Theo Bréjaart
P.O. Box 5199
3008 AD Rotterdam

New Zealand

Peter McLeavey
PO Box 69.007
Auckland

West Germany

Der Fenster Laden
Berliner Str 8
D 6483 Bad Soden
Salmunster

126

P.P. Hempel
Ortolangweg 34
1000 Berlin 47

Heikona De Ruijter
Kloeppelgrosshandel
Langer Steinweg 38
D4933 Blomberg

Sources of Information

The Lace Guild
The Hollies
53 Audnam
Stourbridge
West Midlands
DY8 4AE

The Lace Society
Linwood
Stratford Road
Oversley
Alcester
Warwickshire
BY9 6PG

The British College of Lace
21 Hillmorton Road
Rugby
Warwickshire
CV22 5DF

The English Lace School
Oak House
Church Stile
Woodbury
Nr Exeter

International Old Lacers
President
Gunvor Jorgensen
366 Bradley Avenue
Northvale
NJ 076647
United States

United Kingdom Director of International
  Old Lacers
S. Hurst
4 Dollius Road
London
N31 RG

Further Reading

DEVONIA, *The Honiton Lace Book*, (The Bazaar Office, London, first published 1873; reprinted by Paul Minet, London, 1972)

LUXTON, ELSIE, *The Technique of Honiton Lace*, (B. T. Batsford Ltd, first published 1979)

LUXTON, ELSIE, *Honiton Lace Patterns*, (B.T. Batsford Ltd, first published 1983)

MAIDMENT, MARGARET, *A Manual of Hand-Made Bobbin Lace*, (Batsford 1931, 1983) reprinted by Piccadilly Rare Books, Paul Minet, London)

PALLISER, *The History of Lace*, (E. P. Publishing Ltd, first published 1902)

PENDERAL MOODY A., *Devon Pillow Lace*, (Cassell & Co Ltd, first published 1907)

TREADWIN, *Antique Point and Honiton Lace*, (Ward Lock & Tyler, London, first published 1874)